To Maggie
all the
best
for
Ron x

Introduction

It's an honest truth that most people have a fairly normal childhood.   Like most children, I assumed my own was normal, but I guess looking back it must have been hard for my mother bringing up six kids, especially with very little income.

I was born on the 24th September, 1965 in a small country town called Banff in the north east of Scotland. On that day my mother got quite a shock. She wasn't expecting two children to come from her womb, especially me. She knew one of her children would be a girl, but then out I came thirty minutes later. She had already thought of a girl's name and had no idea what to call me, so I was named Ronald Lees White (after the doctor who delivered me).

I also remember my mother having lots of visitors to the house. They often brought clothes, which confused me, as the people would eventually come and take them back. I later found out that my mother had the skill of being a seamstress and that was her way of making income for the family. I could not think of anything worse than bringing up six children all alone, but that was what she did. Three were from a previous husband who had died, a victim of a hit and run. Then, of course, there was my father, who would visit regularly in the beginning and when I reached the age of five, no longer had any contact with us.

My older sister was the workhorse of the family; the fiery red head. She disciplined my sister and me and would babysit us when my mother went to the Bingo. I suspect when my father came to the house he was continually confronted by this young woman who stood her ground and said you're not welcome here, go away, or words to that effect. Perhaps that had an influence on why he stopped coming around.

There were times when my mother came home and said she had a shout (a win) and depending on the size we always had a sweetie or the batter from her fish or chicken.

I had two elder brothers, both of who I looked up to. The older one was quite easy to wind up and was most always at his grandmother's house. We rarely saw him.

Then there was my second older brother who sort of taught me to be hard and competitive. He was a natural athlete, loved sports, and was always playing football, golf, or any sport he could adapt to — he was a good all-rounder. He taught me how to play everything and I would practice constantly, so much so that my mother would shout, "Your dinner is ready!" and by the time I appeared it would be so cold, I could hardly eat it.

I remember my mother taking me and my sister to the local church to get baptized (Church of Scotland). The minister said he did not have time that particular day, and I can recall my mother having a heated argument. When I was older, my mother told me that she had told the minister to stick religion up his ass. I guess, to this day that is my view on the subject; religion was only invented to suppress people and control them. So when people ask me what my religious views are, I always say football (soccer). When you think about it, a sport can bring so many people together and there is peace and harmony, unless of course it's the 'old firm', but I'll talk about in a later chapter.

I don't think many people have many recollections about their childhood, but a particular one stands out in my mind and had a tremendous effect on me. I remember it had been raining, something that it does every day in Scotland. I was wearing my wellie boots and came in from the rain and was bored. I liked playing in the rain, but this particular day was a torrential downpour. My mother had been knitting and she was preparing supper. Me, being my usual mischievous self, picked up the knitting needles. I was sticking them in the electric socket and, low and behold, I found myself flying through the air. My sister shot out of her chair and I know she must have seen the look of panic on my face. If I hadn't been wearing those wellies, I probably wouldn't be writing this book. I was extremely lucky!!!

Chapter 1

Jackets For Goalposts

The general rules for Parkie and School playground football are as follows:

The object is to force the ball between two large, unkempt piles of jackets (goalposts).

As the sides increase, so do the heaps. Each jacket added to the pile by a new addition to a side should be placed on the inside nearest the goalkeeper, thus reducing the target area.

It is also important that the sleeve of one of the jackets should stick out across the goalmouth, as it will often be claimed that the ball went "over the post".

The on-going reduction of the size of the goal is the responsibility of any respectable defense.

In the absence of a crossbar, the upper limit of the target area is observed as being slightly above head height. This is down to the discretion of the goalkeeper and usually resolved by the best fighter – he always has the final say.

There are no pitch markings. Instead, physical objects denote the boundaries, ranging from the most common - walls and buildings - to roads or kerbs.

Corners and throw-ins where a two-story building or a six-foot granite wall denotes bylines or touchlines. Instead, a scrum should be instigated to decide possession. The three corners penalty rule almost always applies.

The goalkeeper should also try not to be distracted by the inevitable fighting that has, by this point, broken out.

The Ball or Balloon is almost always supplied by the kid with no mates, he is desperate to have friends, so he asks his parents to spend their life savings on the best 'mitre delta'.

There are a variety of types of ball approved for Primary School Football. I shall describe three notable examples.

The plastic balloon. An extremely lightweight model, used primarily in the early part of the season and seldom after that due to having burst. Disadvantages: over-susceptible to influence of the wind, difficult to control, and almost magnetically drawn to flat school roofs whence never to return.

The rough-finish Mitre. Half football, with the panels coming off and the bladder sticking out. Advantages: looks quite grown up, makes for high-scoring matches (keepers won't even attempt to catch it). Disadvantages: scars or maims anything it touches.

Picture the scene. Ball over the wall or on school roof. No added time for stoppages, for whoever put it over had to go and get it. The retriever risked life and limb to scale the drainpipe or negotiate the barbed wire in order to return the ball to play. I remember many occasions when some unsuspecting kid scaling the wall fell waist deep in an oil drum full of water that was behind the school dyke. This, of course, was in block C. That wall was a challenge in itself.

This was playground football at its finest!

The matches were carried on during break time, sometimes with additional players. The game was played on the playground surface of tarmacadam.

Bigger boys would also steal your ball, especially if you had a new one. Our playground was ruled by Newton, a highly irritating school bully who would threaten people with a good kick-in if they tackled him.

The funny part was always picking sides. I was quite a handy goalkeeper and was generally always picked first. I remember getting asked to play in goals when I was 13 for the under 16's in the Deveronvale gala. We won that final and Newton was the captain, of course.

The Duration for matches are as follows;

Matches shall be played over three unequal periods: two playtimes and lunchtime.

Each of these periods shall begin shortly after the ringing of a bell, and although a bell is also rung towards the end of these periods, play may continue for up to ten minutes afterwards, depending on the "bottle" of the participants with regard to corporal punishment met out to latecomers back to the classroom.

When the bell rings there is a sliding scale of kids joining the line, those who stand in line as soon as the bell rings, known as "poofs", and finally to those who will hang on until a teacher actually has to physically retrieve them, known as "bams".

It is important, therefore, in picking the sides, to achieve a fair balance of poofs and bams in order that the score line is achieved over a sustained period of play.

The score line to be carried over from the previous period of the match is in the trust of the last bams to leave the field of play, and may be the matter of some debate.

The matches would continue after school, with different teams of course. We had mini leagues: Malcolm Roaders/ Cramond Terracers / Smith Roaders / Kingswell Parkers. In the summer these games would either end in fights or by a Menopausal old bag confiscating the ball and putting a knife through it or calling the police. I am sure this is one of the reasons why the signs went up saying no football in park areas. This was the death of our community.

Another funny thing was the Celebration; I used to imagine I was Kenny Daglish when I scored a goal, a famous Celtic/Liverpool forward and prolific striker in his day.

The Smith Roaders:

Mikie Duncan-Davie Riddel-Newton-Andy Main-George Duncan-Aldie Duncan-Sedaka and John Stewart (Mincer was the sub)-Gary Paterson-Stuart Paterson (Best Mate)

The Malcolm Roaders:

Me (in goal or striker) Gordon Shepard-Duncan Shepard-David Wilson (Dinky)- Paul Mcalister (Soles) Howard Winton (Howie) Martin Duncan- Kevin Duncan

Cramond Terracers

Gus- Mikie Rithcie-Kevin Ritchie-Billy Gregor-Ian Gregor-Scott Crocket-Alan Masson.

Kingswell Parkers

Arnold Duncan-David Smith- Frankie Day- Barry Wilson- Billy Morrison- Nigel Meldrum. Maxwell Horne.

These guys were the whipping boys and considered the snobs, because they lived in posh houses, the new suburbia. As a footnote, however, it should be stressed that any goal scored by the Best Fighter will be met with universal acclaim. The whole team would leap praise on the team bully, I am not going to name any names, but we all had one on our teams, though maybe not the Kingswell parkers!!

If the game ever reached the Penalty phase, all sorts of rules would be introduced, the sort of make them up as you go along rules. Each side often has one appointed penalty-taker, who will defer to a teammate in special circumstances, such as his requiring one more for a hat trick. The playground side has two appointed penalty-takers: the Best Player and the Best Fighter. The arrangement is simple: the Best Player takes the penalties when his side is a retrievable margin behind, and the Best Fighter at all other times. If the side is comfortably in front, the ball-owner may be invited to take a penalty.

Goalkeepers are often the subject of temporary substitutions at penalties, forced to give up their position.

Offside

There wasn't an offside for two reasons: one, "it's nae' a full-size pitch", and two, none of the players actually know what offside was. The lack of an offside rule gives the option of the goal poachers or glory hunters. They usually players hang around the opposing goalmouth while play carries on at the other end, awaiting a long pass forward out of defense, which they can help past the keeper before running the entire length of the pitch with their arms in the air.

The absence of a referee meant the team bullies usually decided the decisions. This was like a scoring system. I gave you the last one so you would have to give this one, except of course when the street lights would come on, that was the signal for you going home or your mother shouting, it was bath time. When it came to this stage, it was usually pre-planned between teammates, especially if you were leading. If the ball looked in off the post and the other team claimed it, your team would shout no goal and time up. This usually ended in heated arguments.

It was always funny when picking teams. Sometimes they were balanced, more times they were not, especially at school, if you arrived late you would be selected by who had the next pick or depending on your ability.

The first selections will be the two recognized Best Fighters, to ensure a fair balance in the adjudication process, selecting a captain. Special consideration is also given during the selection process to the owner of the ball, depending on the condition of the ball and, of course, the skill.

Chapter 2

School years

My first day at school, I was five years old. I remember walking to school with my mum, sister, and cousin, Barry, and his mother, Elsie. My mother and Elsie were twins also and both were single parents. Although Barry's father was around more than mine; he was in the merchant navy. Barry and me were inseparable, we played together and were always around at each other's house, but mainly I was at his, as his mother would make more for us to eat. We used to be the terrors of the classroom and were always landing each other in trouble. I always managed to do things and got away with almost everything. Barry's mother was always round at our house complaining how I managed to get her son in so much trouble. Eventually, our mothers decided they would limit us being around each other. They tried to stop us from seeing each other in the evening, but during school we were always together. After school we used to go where his mother worked. She was a receptionist at a local car garage, and we would always play football at the adjoining field, Canal Park. Afterwards, we went across to the garage for a hot chocolate from the vending machine.

Primary years were the best times. School at 8.45, playing a little before class; break at 10.30, up the backy for a kick a boot, back to class, and then over to the canteen for school dinners. School dinners were awesome. We tried to compete with each other on how many times we could go up for seconds and thirds. I still can't believe we still had the energy to go and play afterwards. I think today I would be lying down somewhere sleeping. It amazes me the energy we had as kids and we were continually on the go looking for some kind of mischief.

I remember one day in particular I had found an action man toy gun, about the size of a ballpoint pen. I was about eight years old, and I went to some six and seven year olds and told them if I pressed the gun against their arm a needle would come out and they would be injected with poison (what shit kids think of) I guess this could be considered bullying, which am not particularly proud of. God forbid if this happened to my daughter! I supposedly injected around five kids, then went to class. It was during break time that Mr. Espie ventured to the playground (something that he never normally did) and two of the kids whom I had previously injected followed him, both pointing fingers at me. I had been caught. I was summoned for my first visit to the Rectors office and it certainly wouldn't be my last. I was given three strokes of the ruler over my hand, which certainly brought a tear to my eye.

During school, we had a teacher called Mrs. Clark. She used to discipline you by digging her nails into your hand or poking you in the chest. One day, I was in class and we had just got in from break. Barry sat down next to me. I had a girl's eraser and when she started looking for it, I put it on Barry's desk. She dived to grab it and I pushed her on top of my cousin. The desk fell over and when the teacher arrived, she saw them rolling on the floor. Mrs. Clark went berserk and asked him to pick the desk up. He rightly blamed me, and even though I denied everything, he stood his ground. The headmaster was called and my cousin received three of the belt. I guess I felt bad at the time, but I was the green-eyed boy with a cheeky smile and found I could get away with most things.

As a kid, I found myself more and more into sports, playing football as much as I could. Although technically I wasn't the best, there was no substitute for speed. I was the fastest kid in school and I was proud of it. I loved running — it made up for my lack of academic achievements.

What I didn't achieve in the classroom I made up for in the sports field. Our school, Banff Primary, began playing in the inter-primary competition for our district. The league consisted of six teams. I remember playing outfield and our goalkeeper was injured. There was no substitute goalkeeper, so I stepped up. The brother I looked up to was the playing semi-pro goalkeeper for a local team. I guess all the hours of practicing with him paid off. We won that game and I was man of the match and saved a penalty.

I began to catch the eye of some older players and they were soon asking me to be their goalkeeper for their 5-aside teams. I was small, agile, fast, fearless, and most importantly a little bit crazy – as most keepers are..

I remember playing in a local tournament once and a man came up to me and said, "If you stick with it and keep playing as well as you do, you will go a long way." That very guy went on to represent his country and in 1990 World Cup Finals.

The primary school years were flying by and my report cards were not getting any better. My popularity, however, was getting much better. I couldn't wait for break times, and was consistently first up the backy and getting the jackets down, which marked the goals, of course. Even when the older kids got there, they saw my jacket was down and they knew I was a goalkeeper, so I would always play on the top pitch. The bottom pitch was reserved for my classmates and I think they were a bit jealous that I was always at the top pitch.

I remember being bullied when I was in primary 3 by a guy older than me. Every day he made my life hell at lunchtime. For a week, I couldn't avoid him – he hounded me from the moment the bell went off. I was walking to get something from the Vanie (Clarkies, the bakers, had the best cloutie dumplings ever) and the guy was following me. I turned around and punched him right in the face and then kicked him in the stomach. I was reported to the headmaster the next day and I had to explain. He was having none of it and saw me as the instigator. At lunchtime my elder sister came to school and fixed the issue. Suffice to say, the guy never bullied me again.

We left Banff primary in the summer of '76 and although I vaguely remember the time, as I played in my first 5-aside gala that year, my primary school years were a blur academically. I was always told to try harder. I tried hard on the field, but that didn't seem to matter.

Transition. I thought it meant something different, but the year of 1976 it meant another school. This was a school in another town, which brought schools together from rural areas to prep them for high school. For me, this was a chance to show off my sporting skills and try to impress some new girls.

I remember the first break-time, all the guys hanging out together from the same schools, walking around, playing football, marbles, hopscotch, and chasses. I found myself attracted to a large group. I heard this guy saying he had the hardest head in the world! So I asked, "How do you work that out?" He told me to watch then he continued to head-butt this hard wall until his head bled. Because of this, it was collectively thought that he must be one of the toughest characters, so he needed to be on our side. Two weeks later he was in a fight with one girl from our previous school and he lost. I guess he didn't use his head when it came to fighting (not that I condone fighting girls).

The thing I looked forward to most was football practice. It was the first soccer practice and I was keen to impress. When the coach said goalkeepers, four of us stepped forward. I wasn't the tallest, but I was agile and confident. The coach knew one of the goalies, so he was automatically selected. I quickly stepped up to the plate to be selected for the other side. During that practice match, I remember watching the other goalie and thinking, I have a challenge on my hand if I want to play in this position. His positional sense was good and he seemed to control and demand his penalty area well. That was a lesson I certainly learned from: don't focus on others, concentrate on your own game when the match is in duration. I conceded three goals and the other keeper let in one. Maybe it was down to his team having better strikers, but I think he was more focused than me.

When I looked at the team sheet, the following day I saw I had been selected for the second team, which really didn't stop me from getting some stick from my second oldest brother. He always said, "There will always be someone better than you, but the real test is how hungry you are to become better."

I knew I had to perform and practice more, but so did he. I remember watching him first play. His father was always they're watching and encouraging him. I didn't have that.

Well, not till later on in life, but I will talk about that later. All through that schooling year, I never once broke into the position I wanted the most, but I guess that's life sometimes. You can't always have what you want. But what I did have was more trophies from the 5-aside comps we entered throughout that year and the summer gala, four of the five times we met in the 5's our team was the victor. I guess we had the better strikers!

During another time at school, a certain pupil had stolen 20GBP from his mother's purse. Unbeknown to the rest of the pupils standing in line for our break time, he was positioned at the front of the Van and when Crockett (the van driver) asked him what he wanted, he replied, "Everything in the Van." Sweets, Pastries, Juice, Crisps, you name it, he bought it that day. You see, there are certain things that remain implanted in your head, definitely because of the obscurity of it all. I mean, who else would have bought the entire contents of the Van? He wasn't really that popular, but he certainly had his 15 minutes of fame that day. He told everyone to take what they wanted. I was, of course, on a budget and was glad of the extra sweets. Everyone had his or her fair share. During the afternoon, we heard the dreaded tannoy, asking for the very boy to come to the headmistress office to meet with his disgruntled mother, asking about the missing money. I would have loved to be a fly on the wall then, especially when he explained that he bought the vannies contents.

That year passed quickly and by the summer of '77, I was getting ready for high school. More kids, more teachers, and more fun!

There were two things important in my life at that point: playing football and watching football. One team in particular was the object of my attention: Glasgow Celtic (which I will dedicate a whole chapter to). Up until then, I had never saw them live. One player was my childhood hero and become an enemy overnight. He signed for Liverpool for £ 440,000, a British transfer fee at the time, and broke my heart. I ripped all my posters down and became disillusioned with football. How could someone so good walk away from the greatest club in the world?

I decided to follow I walked away from football and began playing a sport that changed my life and opened new doors for me.

Teachers at our school were a pain in the backside. I either found myself getting on well with them or disliking them extremely. I had a crush on my English teacher and spent most of the lesson staring at her, hoping maybe she would notice me. I met her about ten years after leaving school and she was just as charming and perhaps even more attractive than when I was at school. I asked her for a dance, as I was always the cheeky outspoken kid. She accepted, but when I whispered some sweet nothings in her ear, I smelt cigarettes in her hair. I asked her if she smoked. She replied that she did and that was a no-no in my books. It didn't matter who was in front of supermodel, film star, whatever – if they smoke they haven't got a hope in my book.

Boris; Mention this name and everyone who ever attended BXA remember him. He was the teacher from hell from the Math's department. He is perhaps one of the sole reason's why I don't understand Math's.

It was hard enough without having a teacher like this in the department. It takes a lot to scare me; he was one of them. He reminded me of Billy Bunter; small, fat, and round. My guess was that he was either bullied as a child or mentally abused in some shape or form.

On one occasion, during the last day of term, Boris who always wanted to show his prowess for chess, brought out the chessboards. The whole class played chess. Boris would always ask for the best chess players to come forward, but no one generally volunteered, as he would always win. This day was different. Mincer took his A-game and beat him. Mincer let out a celebratory, "Yes!" Boris looked disgruntled, but the rest of the class celebrated. You would have thought Scotland had scored the winner in the world cup final. Boris had steam coming out of his ears. That was when he slowly opened the drawer of his desk, a rehearsal that he had practiced so many times. The class sighed as Mincer stood up and took two of the best on each hand, a great way to celebrate a victory. I mean, originally I think the belt was a deterrent at school; it separated the black sheep from the followers and when used in the right manner, it worked. But to use it as a punishment for someone beating a teacher at chess?

Boris had a real dry sense of humor. I certainly couldn't see him leading a football chant or a demo. He had recognizable phrases he used in every class he taught and follow ups to boot. Quote Number 1: Everybody Answers…. If only two people answer, you, you, you, ten times in ink for tomorrow morning. Number 2: Is it night or day Laddie/Lassie? This was the usual quote when someone went to get their work marked and they had answered wrongly. It questioned whether you were awake and listening to his dulcet tone.

On another occasion a girl who sat at the front of the class was asked to read an equation from the blackboard. She quoted that "nothing point five" (0.5) was the answer. Boris looked around and corrected her, "It's not 'nothing point five' its zero point five." He asked her the question again and she replied with the same answer. This carried on for another two or three times and by that point the whole class was laughing. The girl was so embarrassed, but you could see the rage on Boris's face. He ended up belting her and from that day we realized he didn't like to be intimidated, especially where laughter was concerned.

I'm sure I could write a book on Boris alone, as I had him for four out of my five years in the Academy. I learned not to take him too seriously by the second year. We were sitting in class and James Shayler walked through the door. I knew him from Rugby. We had a double period and it was just before break time when James came in and, as he approached Boris's desk, he threw down his leaving form and said, "Sign this you fat bastard.".... The whole class was in total shock and we all began sniggering. Shayler, continued his outburst saying Boris was the worst teacher on the planet and for four years had made his life total hell. Shayler said he would be glad to see the back of him. Boris looked at him and you could see the steam coming out of his ears. It was then that I realized he was a bully. When we returned from break time, Boris did his usual routine of pulling the board down to prepare for the lesson. Every kid knew his routine of by heart, especially how he used to clean the board, looking around occasionally to try and catch someone unaware who was making faces at him. He wasn't prepared for what he was about to see. He pulled down the board and there was a chalk picture of him. Someone had drawn him and wrote underneath, Boris is a Fat Bastard. The whole class gasped and laughed at the same time. Boris quickly erased the portrait from the board and asked the class if anyone know who did it. There definitely weren't any volunteers raising their hands. I suspected James Shayler went in at break time and did the artful deed, but I suppose only he and his close friends will ever know the truth.

Rugby Years (School)

I remember my cousin saying to me, "Instead of watching the u13's play Football, come to rugby training on Saturday morning. You'll like it!" I arrived and we played a game called touch rugby, which involved no tackling. I quite enjoyed it. My handling skills were quite good, probably because of my goalkeeping skills, when I received the ball I was able to see and find gaps. With my speed I could get past players with ease and could create space. I must admit, I enjoyed my first training session and couldn't wait till the next one.

When I look back, knowing what I have learned about fitness over the years, the Physical educational teachers at school were pretty average. They gave you a ball and put you outside in the rain, whilst they stayed inside watching TV, smoking, and having a cup of coffee. What a life! It's only when the lesson had to come indoors, especially during the hard winter months or snow days, when the pitches were frozen for some weeks that you began to see the true worth of your PE teacher. Mr. Martin was a proud individual that most people disliked, not because of his ability as a teacher, but more because of his discipline levels. He was educated at Loughborough and was a half decent rugby player who played for the local team. He would line us up during the lesson and ask questions. More than anything, he hated watching his classes being turned into a rip fest. I used to try my hardest and push him to the brink during every lesson. I remember on one occasion when we were playing basketball, one player in particular stood out. He would take the ball, dribble the court pass, receive, shoot, and score. This was beginning to piss me off and even more so when Mr. Martin gave him lots of credit. Looking back, I understand he was getting his own back at me, because he knew what would get to me. On the guy's next attack I traced his tall spectacled frame and as he passed and waited for the return. I lurked behind him, like a cat waiting to spring on a bird. He jumped and I pushed him as hard as I could in the middle of his back. I can still see his specs spinning across the floor and the lens falling out and Mr. Martin screaming at the top of his voice, "Ron! My office, now!" The kids went into a chorus of, "Ooooo's." I still had the cheeky smile on my face. When I reached the office, I was given a lecture on sportsmanship, discipline, manners, and behavior, all of which I didn't get high marks for. But after hearing he was going to have to belt me, I certainly began to think on how to behave during his class. While in school I received the belt around 20 times and Mr. Martin was definitely in the top two. That day, he reduced me to tears. I was a 13 year old crying in the toilet and afterwards, I walked into class with a not so cheeky smile. I am all for corporal punishment in schools as long as it's for a good reason. It's a deterrent and teaches the children to become more disciplined and behave properly in some lessons. On the other hand, some teachers would use it just for the sake of it and not for the intended use. I certainly behaved myself in his class after that day.

Although Mr. Martin was our PE teacher, he was the Rugby coach for the senior team. He was the man who brought our school to the front of school rugby to the point where only the posh schools could compete. He nurtured raw talent into players that would fight for themselves as well as the cause. His U16 sides were champions of the north of Scotland and six of the players were in the North midlands select side. I wanted that; popularity and, most of all, recognition as something more than a prankster.

My coach was more like a father figure to someone and me whom, to this day; I hold the utmost respect for. He was a geography teacher by day and an Athlete by night, well on the rugby field, anyway. He was a hooker (no 2), a term used in rugby for a person that is in the front row of the scrum. He turned me into a player that could use speed to deadly ability and pushed me harder and harder, challenged me more and more. I couldn't get enough sprints, runs, kicking, or running. I loved every minute and he would challenge me more and more. What I didn't realize he was nurturing me to achieve greater things. Soon, I was ready for my first game against IRA (Inverness Royal Academy). It was an Autumnal morning, the kind of morning you knew in Rugby season where the grass was freshly cut and smelled, as only the people who played in those conditions would remember. I was on the wing and we were leading 6-4 with two minutes to go. Their winger caught me flat footed and was sprinting to the corner. I could only catch him one way and that was what I did, I slid tackled him and clipped his boots with my foot (which is totally illegal). Down he went like a sack of potatoes and that almost ended my Rugby career. Mr. Martin was ref and he was adamant I would never represent the school at any level again! My coach, George, did a lot of begging and apologizing for my conduct. Fortunately, I was the likable rogue and a character he liked in the team. I probably had more confidence because I hung around with older boys than myself. I suppose that came from playing football.

I was banned from playing for three weeks, which looking back didn't seem too bad, but at the time it seemed like an eternity. I stayed not too far from the rugby pitches, so I went and practiced place kicking and goal kicking as maybe one day my services would be required. My first game back was against Gordonstoun, a public school which Prince Charles and his brother, Edward, attended. Our team played against Edward and he was driven to the pitch in a separate vehicle along with four bodyguards. Wow! We were amazed. We hammered them that day and in true rugby and posh boy's fashion they were bemused at how a team of commoners could defeat such gents. I ran in three tries and was man of the match. I guess I had a point to prove and Mr. Martin even patted me on the back. George gave me the usual nod of the head, and told me to keep my feet on the ground. I replied, "Ok, Dad!"

We were top of the league going into the final game. We had an away fixture, a bus trip with the seniors, and time to impress. I sat with my cousin and we were looking for opportunities to outdo each other as we approached the town. I saw two nuns in the distance; now was my opportunity to impress. I pulled my trousers down and flashed my white ass at the two Nuns. The whole bus erupted with laughter and the two coaches looked round, bemused with the situation. We came, we played, we conquered, and we sinned that day. And we sung *We Are*

the Champions, as the U13, U15 were school district
winners.

On Monday morning, we were summoned to the school
assembly hall and we thought it was going to be a briefing
on how to conduct ourselves when receiving the trophy
from the headmaster. How wrong we were. Out came Mr.
Martin, George, and Mr. Moncrief, the assistant rector.
First, the latter congratulated the teams on their success
on the field, then he followed by saying "There was an
incident where certain individuals on the bus mooned
their bottom to two innocent nuns, tarnishing the
reputation of our school." George looked at me in the way
my mother used too when I did something wrong. Had any
of the seniors said something? I knew it wasn't any of our
guys, as playing team sports like rugby, everyone would
stick together. It was time to bite the bullet. I decided to
step forward and face the music. I could have bluffed my
way out of it, but there was no point. I just had to accept
the fact I did wrong. All the kids were asked to leave and I
was summoned to the assistant head's office along with
George. This was the time I knew George was the real
father figure in my life. He said, "Ron is a great rugby
player, someone who reminds me of a great soccer player,
Jimmy Johnstone." He was the guy involved in a rowing
boat incident, who had been pushed out into a lake with
no oars and very drunk. "He is a likable character,
someone who is really important to the team." How could
someone say something like this? I expected it from my
mother, but from a teacher whom I had only known for
one year?! Mr. Moncrief replied, "I can understand where
you are coming from, Mr. Webster, but to tarnish the
school's reputation – that is more heinous!" George was
asked to leave. My father figure disappeared! "Have you

anything to say about the matter?" I was asked. I thought for a few minutes and replied, "I am sorry for what I did, I was just trying to impress the seniors and never thought about the school. Does this mean I can't play rugby again?" Mr. Moncrief replied that it was up to Mr. Martin and Mr. Webster to decide. He then asked what my position was on the Rugby field. I replied 11 or 14, but I would like to be 10. He said if I had been belted this year, I and I told him, once or twice. He said, "If you're not sure then perhaps you don't remember the other times. You will certainly remember this occasion, though."

I received three of the best and I can honestly say, there was tears running down my cheeks. The pain was hell, my hands were stinging' it felt like I had just put them in ice cold water, I ran to the toilets and let lukewarm water run over them to dull the pain.

I started to ask myself where was my guidance growing up, I had no father figure. I couldn't blame my mother, as she had enough on her plate. Maybe it was because I never had much attention and the only way I could express myself was by doing things like this. These types of actions probably made me resent my father even more. I haven't spoken too much about my father but there are certain things that spring to mind. I remember walking up past his local bar on many occasions and seeing him propped against the bar with a half decker and a chaser and occasionally he would see me, come out, and offer me some money. I just would walk away, and ignore him. I have never been a drinker or a smoker. I tend to think there are more pleasurable things to spend your money on, rather than waste them on vices that are no good for you.

What will I do without Rugby, I thought? I knew I would miss the feeling of belonging to something and maybe achieving some recognition. I went to the PE department to meet with George and Mr. Martin. I was asked to wait outside and I thought, *why does this always happen to me?* It made me resent my father more and more. I went into the office and the first thing Mr. Martin said to me was, "Give me one good reason why I should still let you carry on playing Rugby." I thought for a while and I looked at George and said, "I have been brought up by my mother because my father was never around. The only father figure I have is that man sitting there." I think by the look on their faces they were not expecting an answer like that. I was asked to leave the office. Maybe they had already decided and after that answer, maybe they would let me stay. The five minutes that passed seemed like an eternity. Finally, they came out. George was smiling and I knew the outcome. Mr. Martin said, "We have decided to give you one more chance. Don't let the school or your coach down."

When I left the office I was on cloud nine. Most of friends thought I would be out as well. When I met with them at break time they were as happy as me. They said the practical jokes and training wouldn't have been the same without me. We had a good bunch of guys in the team, full of character, and the banter was always flowing.

One game in particular in in Stonehaven, we arrived two hours before KO, and my cousin and me went for a walk in the grounds. We came across the headmasters office and sitting on the inside windowsill was the school mascot, a teddy bear monkey dressed in the school colors. The first thing that came to mind was, that would be a great souvenir! Then I thought if we were caught I definitely would be out of the team. I told my cousin to get it, so he did. The door was ajar and he went in and was out in a flash, monkey in hand. I opened my bag and stuffed it straight in. That very evening I said to my cousin, "Let's meet at the local chip shop and we will impress the girls with our monkey story." I told them the monkey was real and they were sort of believing it, though I think the only monkeys we were likely to see was in a Tarzan movie. I went up to my house and got the monkey and put my dog's lead on it, then walked it down to the chip shop. The girls believed the whole story and it was only when one of them got a close look that our cover was blown. It was funny while it lasted and it passed another boring evening in the small town I grew up in.

At least we didn't receive the dreaded tannoy announcement on returning to school on Monday morning. This time our pranks had taken place with no punishment. Mondays were like working days, as I would find out, as I grew older. Not much to look forward to, but definitely glad when they're over. Our registration teacher for the next two and a half years would be a certain English teacher, Mr. Shand. He was also very much into soccer, but had a love affair with a rival team I supported. I would find myself getting into many arguments with Mr. Shand, especially as every essay I wrote was related to Glasgow Celtic. I knew so much about the club, it was scary. I had spent nearly all my money following the club and buying stuff.

Mr. Shand used to say if there was a topic, which I could relate to Celtic for my exam paper, and then I would have no problem passing the exam.

Rugby was becoming more and more enjoyable and when the 5 nations (now 6) came on TV, we would find ourselves cheering for the Scots with a passion. We loved the players, like Andy Irvine, John Rutherford, Jim Renwick, and, of course, Roy Laidlaw, a small guy with a big heart! I used to dream one day I would pull on the famous blue shirt of the Scots. I remember the school organizing a trip to Aberdeen, where the North Midlands were playing the All Blacks. Wow! We were all excited and we really thought we had a chance of beating them. I looked at the team list in the program and found only one squad player in the Scottish line up! I was to find out during my senior playing career, this was the great North/South divide. A second string All Black side beat North midlands convincingly. Again, the gulf between to small nations was on show. I had set myself a goal and to get there I had to train hard and practice more, but there were obstacles in my way, mainly from the other shaped ball, that of football. I found myself playing football again and at the age of 14, playing outside right (Right wing) for a local amateur side that played in the summer league, so it did not clash with the winter sport of Rugby. Although technically I was not very gifted, I had speed and all I would do is knock the ball past opponents or either crossed to my waiting striker, Paul Mac, a player who was lighting quick and had a great physique. He was so powerful and had the heart of a lion. We became real good friends. He was a few years older than me, a ladies man; I think they all wanted to get their hands on his body. I found when playing football, it was easier to pick up injuries. Although a contact sport, sometimes your body was not aware of contact, you could skip past an opponent but two seconds later, bang! You were turned over. That rarely happened in Rugby. When I went past someone, it was like showing some a clean pair of heels. By the time they adjusted their body to tackle, I was past them. In football, if you passed someone, they lunged at you from behind and stretched a leg out. Your body is less aware for that. Our small town of Banff was a typical town in the late 70's early 80's; many characters lived here. The men were typical men of the era, working class guys who spent there time in bars and going home to their wives, with their salary spent. My grandfather was a farmer who died before I was born, so I never had that father figure in my life. What I never really understood was why my father wasn't around for us in the early years. I now see these type of fathers as wasters, all they did was live for the pub and the banter. 'The banter' was part and parcel of growing up in the town, if you could take the banter and dishes it out, then that was half the battle. I loved the banter and I suppose growing up with older mates made me sharper when the banter was flowing. I sometimes used to lay in bed thinking about quick-witted comebacks.

The other good thing about playing football, apart from being played in summer, was the school holidays. My mother would sometimes come to watch, but if we had a final she would definitely come. Most of the other players had their fathers watching. I never even looked for mine. Why should I? We were playing really well that season and we had reached the final and the whole town was talking about the match. The other team, Macduff, was our archrivals, second in the league and, although an older more experienced side, we were the side that had youth and talent. When I arrived for that match, the crowd was beginning to line the sidelines. When we came out for the warm up I heard someone shout my name, "Ron, whitey, Ron!" I looked across and I saw my father and wondered why he was there. Then it dawned on me, the game was sponsored by the local whisky distillery where he worked (drank most of his wages). I ignored him and focused on the match ahead. In the dressing room, our manager came in and seemed very nervous. He was giving us instructions and I piped up and asked him what he was looking so nervous about. I told him to just give the ball to me and I will get past that slow left back of theirs. He said, we all know what you can do, but it's the guys on the other team I am frightened about. I suppose this was his way of firing up the boys. When we came out of the dressing room, I couldn't believe the amount of people who had showed up. We were 20 minutes into the game, I got the ball on the right and skipped past their slug of a left back and crossed it for Paul to score. I rubbed the head of the left back and said next time; I would send him a postcard. He was furious. I was giving him a torrid time, turning him inside out. I had him in my hipper, terms for making a fool of someone on the football pitch. I received the ball again and I was past him, cut inside, and stroked the ball into the corner of the net. You could see the players' heads were down.

At half time, Bill, our manager, said, "Watch yourself, Ron, he will be out to nail you in the second half." To nail someone is to deliberately injure them. I would never do that in a football or Rugby match, so I guess I didn't really understand. I had the ball at my feet 10 minutes into the second half, went to go past the left back again, then bang, a two footed tackle and my game was over. He received yellow and was substituted 10 minutes after. I was sitting on the touchline with an ice pack and my father came up and said, "Are you alright son? It looked like a bad one." I replied, "Fit do you care anyway?" We won the cup 3-1 and all the guys were happy as I stood up and walked over to shake the left back's hand. He pushed me away. I don't know where my father came from, but he ran at the guy. I stepped in, well hobbled, and said, "I don't need you to fight my battles, you have never been around for me in the past and as far as am concerned you are as big a loser as that tosser that fouled me." I was never a guy to mince my words. I have always say what's on my mind, I find it's better out in the open. I dislike people who cheat and lie to get somewhere and who take things away from people who deserve it more than they do. My season was over with badly torn ligaments and we had two weeks until school went back. I was two months away from my 15th birthday and going into third year, make or break year, as this was pre-lims. Returning to school and arranging my timetable for the year ahead was always a challenge, especially as I was only sitting 6 O grades, so filling the spaces was going to be a problem. I found myself taking classes that were of no interest to me and the only period I looked forward to was PE, I needed my sports kit for every day of the week. On the weekend, I played Rugby and football, so my mother was always cleaning my sports kit.

The rugby season was soon starting again and the Autumnal smells were flowing through the fresh air. The smell of the last cut of grass and the aroma of decomposing leaves were the telltale signs of Rugby season. The first training session was always interesting, I was one of the smallest players in the side and my growth seemed to stunt while all the other guys had grown. This did not stop me from running away from them, as I played football during the summer months, so my fitness was beginning to show. I was sharp and first to the ball and breaking through defense was easy for me. Mr. Webster was giving me more and more drills, the other players who

stood out in our team were, Stuart Dennistoun (Denny),
Johnny Riddell (Riddell), and Barry Wilson (Baz). Denny
was one of the best tacklers I had ever seen. He was
fearless and quick; he was our last line of defense at
fullback and you could rely on him for taking the last man
down. Riddell was our front row, he came from a family of
stock car drivers and was driving and repairing cars since
he was 13 years old. In the good old days of ruck and maul,
he would go into the ruck and all you would hear was
johnny's baw, and 9.5 times out of 10 he came out of that
ruck with the ball. An extremely strong player, with a quick
turn of pace, but unfortunately it only would last for 10
meters. Then there was Barry Wilson (my cousin) he was a
tall and strong number eight with a quick turn of pace and
because I knew him, I would always be on his tail. I found
myself being set up by him so many times on the field it
was too good to be true.

The weekend was the time when we got up to the most
mischief. We were playing rugby away from home against
a team called 'Mackie Rfc'. They were a strong U18 team,
but there were no match for us. It was the semi-final of
the North of Scotland. We won the game and decided we
would celebrate, which meant acquiring a souvenir. The
school mascot was spotted in the headmaster's office. It
was a monkey bur it looked real, like the scarecrow. I told
my sister to call her friends and tell them the monkey was
real, then I took my dog's lead and collar, placed them
both around the monkey's neck, and off we went. All the
girls were looking out from the window and we pretended
we had a dancing monkey on a lead. The girls were not
allowed out, if they did we would go home and they
wouldn't get to play with it. When they found out it wasn't

real, after 30 minutes, they laughed and couldn't believe they had been duped

This was the year for selection for North Midlands, a chance to compete against the big boys from the South of Scotland, with the prospect of playing at international level. I was excited going to the first trial in Aberdeen, seven were sent through from Banff and four were invited back: the three and myself mentioned were good choices for the North Midlands. The next session we were cut down to two fifteen asides. We were all played out of position and we were not asked back, I spoke with Mr. Webster, confused about the selection process. He explained, "It's the great north/south divide. Unless you are an exceptional talent, you would not be selected, as it has to do with traveling expenses."

Basically, the SRU did not want to pay for us country boys to travel 45 miles two times a week for training and, if selected for Scotland, 180 miles for training and playing. This would haunt me for the next year and a half and also left me disheartened by the sport I had grown to love.

I was finding it hard to concentrate at school and my studies were suffering. I had a math's teacher who was a nightmare; my housemaster suggested I take extra periods of math's to fill my timetable. I found myself struggling to come to terms with a teacher who was a bully.

Rugby training was becoming harder and harder. The boys were growing and tackling was my weakness. I was always going too high and the players were managing to elude me. When I played alongside Denny, he could always cover for me. He took the knocks and made the passes and I would take the glory of scoring.

Filling the timetable was becoming a chore and extra math's wasn't my cup of tea. I found myself skipping school, something that I didn't like doing as I missed sport. I needed my PE kit every day of the week. It worries me that nowadays kids are becoming really lazy, the emphasis at school is to perform educationally – not to excel at sport. When I look at kids now, I see 50% that I would not like to be on my team. When I was in school, it would have been more like 5%. It's a scary thought that all this happened in only 35 years and this will only get worse, to, unless governments do something about it.

When I finally decided to leave school, the first person I should have informed was my father figure – Coach George. The first time he heard about it was when I went to have my leaving form signed. You would have thought he was reading the death certificate of a family member. He looked at me and said, "You know, I had plans for you this year." *Plans*, I thought, *what could they possible be?* "You could have represented not only your school for rugby, but your country," he finished. When I look back on all the time and effort he spent nurturing me, I can feel and understand his disappointment.

Under 16 Discos at Banff Town Hall on a Friday evening, a place everyone could let there hair down (when I had hair), Girls walking in groups, going in one direction and guys walking in the other, its strange when you look back on such habits.

I think everyone has a hero when they're growing up, especially when they reach 16/17, at the stage when they think they know it all. We all can relate with these times.

Heavy Metal and Rock was my era and Angus Young was my Hero. AC/DC the BEST SCOTTISH BAND TO COME OUT OF AUSTRALIA (I know that statement will wind a lot of Aussies up, but hey ho you don't forget your birth country, especially if you are Scottish) Although AC/DC were my favorite band, there were many bands around equally as good and made famous from the 'Axe Attack' LP's. I think everyone who was into rock had purchased or borrowed an Axe Attack Album.

Iron Maiden and a track called 'The Number of the Beast'. This track was a great floor filler, at our local under 16's Disco at Banff Town Hall. On a Friday evening, with 'Starlight Sandy' spinning the 33's and 45's, if he wanted the floor emptied he played "Walk of Life' by Dire Straits. If he wanted it full he played 'Paradise by the Dashboard Light' by Meat Loaf.

This was what we had to look forward to on a Friday night. Saturdays and Sunday were usually quite boring. We used to hang about at the different venues, Duncan St Chippie, Spar, VG, Coop, or Freddie's. One night at Freddie's, we were watching a horror movie through the back in his café. We used to gather there and watch movies, another place to practice our tonsil tennis with our girlfriends. After the movie we decided to carry on the horror theme and go down to Duff House. This was all pre-planned of course. Two of the guys said they were going home as they had work the next day, but what they did was go the opposite way and met us halfway through the grounds. As me and two other guys started walking into the forest (grounds) there were three girls with us, my girlfriend at the time - Carole, my sister, and Lorraine. I was telling all the creepy stories, suggesting something was there, only an excuse for Carole to get closer (ha ha) then I said, "Look what's that?" They were all shitting themselves, then Lugs (Gordon Mair) the guy who had driven off in his car started playing *The Number Of The Beast*, for those who don't know the song, there is a verse that reads, 'Woe to you oh earth and sea, for the Devil sends the beast with wrath let him who hath understanding recognize the Number of the BEAST' and goes on to the music. Once the girls heard this, they started screaming. I'm sure they still have trauma to this day about that evening, I used to love doing that sort of harmless fun.

Back row. Callum Webster, Malcom Mcallister, Steven Gallon, Barry Wilson.
Middle Row: Dave Reid, David Cant, Gordon Shephard, Robert Sievwright, Alex Mchattie (bariele), Stuart Denniston, Teacher: Campbell Dickson
Front Row: Gary Cox, Andrew Gibson, Ronald Simpson, Grant Robertson, Ron White, Kenneth Duthie , John Riddell

Chapter 3

Leaving School and Having a Laugh

Banff Swimming was my first job when I left school on July 1982 and decided to follow my passion – sport. I got my first paid job on the youth opportunity program (Y.O.P) , which was a government funded program that encouraged employers to take on extra staff and pay them the minimum wage. Because my mother was a single parent, I decided to help her around the house. I was a breadwinner now and paid her for my keep.

I started work at the tender age of 17 and soon began to learn about banter in the workplace, giving it out and taking it back all in my stride. Although the YOP Program was only for six months, I must admit I enjoyed the experience and had a really good rapport with the cleaning lady. She had three girls and I suppose I was like the son she never had! In the summer she would always come in early so she would have more time to spend with her girls. One-day the manager's son, Gary, who also liked playing pranks, and me hatched a plan. We left the front door open as usual. She came through the door to see Gary hanging from a makeshift noose, from the diving board and me sitting beside him laughing. She let out a big scream and ran as fast as she could out of the building. I ran to the foyer window and saw her running down the street. I am surprised she didn't have a heart attack! I caught her before she reached the end of the street and, almost pissing my pants, explained to her it was only a joke.

Although I got on well with the manager at that time, I could see he was grooming me for another role. I liked swimming and he encouraged me to sit in on the swimming lessons. After one lesson, he had me guiding the non-swimmers and encouraging them to put their faces in the water, blow bubbles, etc. etc. By the end of the day I was teaching the whole class. Talk about getting thrown into the deep end! He said, "If you can do this for one week, teaching one class a day without complaint, I promise you when a position is available the job will be yours."

Six months came and went and the position never really materialized.
I like to look at things, a judge people how they judge you; I love when they ask you to grow up! They have either led a boring life or are surrounded by negative and boring people.

When I was 17 I recall babysitting with a friend and being told by the friend, the mother wanted me to stay as she thought I was cute and funny, the women called Liz, showed me things that evening that would put me in good stead for my later years, she was 34 years old, not to say I felt happy when I left her house in the morning.

I haven't really mentioned my father before now, but he was a 'jack the lad' and an alcoholic. I decided that alcohol wasn't really for me and it became more of a social thing. I never even had a drink until my eighteenth birthday. I can remember getting drunk and being sick and not feeling too well the next day, so it wasn't really for me. Whenever I went out for social drinking, I would get to the stage when I knew I had drank enough, usually after 8-10 beers and then I stopped and the silver tongue took over. All the girls in my town were wary of my womanizing ways – I was more likely to break their hearts and leave them. I guess I had adopted some of my father's traits, but I wasn't about to adopt the drinking habits. The more I saw him, the more I began to dislike him. I would walk past his local pub and see him perched in his usual place, cigarette in hand, beer in the other, and some women hanging around him. He sometimes caught a glimpse of me and came running out of the bar, shouting at me, "Far you gan!" I would either walk faster or run away. I imagine he went back into the bar and said, "That's a stubborn one that, but I'm sure one day he will come round." I am 50 years old now and still have not come around.

I also remember going to other towns for a spin, which meant looking for new girls to talk to. When we saw nothing that took our fancy we would take the back roads home and it was on one of these evenings something really funny happened. We were driving past a field of barely and something caught my eye. I said, "Stop, there is a mannie in the field." When we went back there was a scarecrow. We drove back to our town with the scarecrow in the front seat. I was amazed how realistic the scarecrow looked. We drove to the top of the town and took it out of the car and placed it on the road. Then we started to pretend to beat it up. Many cars looked, but never stopped. Then a car finally stopped and we dived into our car and drove off. It was funny seeing people's reactions, but we needed to fuel our excitement. I had an idea to take it down to the local river, which ran between the two towns, where on most summer evenings, tides permitting, fishermen would gather to try and catch a 15lb salmon or the like. I held the scarecrow's legs and shouted, "I'm going to jump of the bridge!" My cousin pretended to be the calming influence and said, "Please don't jump." The fishermen started to take interest and were observing the situation. This was the audience we were looking for. They began to return the call, yelling, "Don't jump!" I continued returning calls until eventually I released the scarecrow's legs and it fell into the water. The fishermen came running across with their waders (giant Wellington boots) and pulled the scarecrow out of the water. We were almost crying with laughter. Then we heard, "Why don't you kids just grow up?" We loved that shout and it only inspired us to do more and more pranks.

Prince Albert

When I was in my teens, I started to hang around with guys older than me and I guess being around them made me feel more mature. Somehow my mother would always trust me when I was with these guys, but if she knew what I was getting up to, then I guess it would've been different. Picture early mornings delivering daily papers and seeing opened garages and looking in them and finding an Aladdin's cave. One particular time, we found or stole a bust of Prince Albert. It weighed around 10kg, slightly more than a full paper bag. We briefly discussed what we were going to do with it. We decided to put it on top of the Mercat cross, a monument in the center of our town. The local press started to take interest in it and was soon taking pictures. The next day, the headlines read 'Who put prince Albert on his steeple?' We used to hang around the local fish and chip shop (Freddies) and play Space Invaders, Pac man, Asteroids, and Defender. If I think about the amount of money we plugged into those machines...

We decided to write a poem about Albert on his steeple. It read: To all you bammfic people/ we know who put Albert on his steeple/ if you want to know then you have not too far to go/ if you venture along the street you will find us at Freddies eats.

We wrote this down on a piece of cardboard and erected it on the steeple that very evening. Two days later, it was on the front page and there were reporters hanging around the chip shop. We were becoming celebrities amongst ourselves and some people were beginning to get jealous of our front-page exploits. The very next day, the bust was taken down and smashed not too far away from the very steeple he proudly occupied for three days. We had a hunch to the person who took it and, without naming anybody; it was a guy with webbed fingers. There's a clue! We liked our fame and we decided to write a poem to grab the headlines once more, it read: to all bammfic people please return Albert to his steeple/ we have a clue who you are and you are as popular as a fish in a jar/ we received our moments of fame it's a shame you are to blame. We told the reporters where we took the bust from and then we went to apologize to the old man. He didn't have a clue it had been removed as he had so much clutter in his garage.

Strawberry picking

Most people pick strawberries for extra pocket money, but we used to pick them for our own consumption. In the summer months, people used to grow strawberries in their back garden, the telltale sign was the green universal net and when I delivered morning papers to people's houses, I was always on the lookout for the green net. One early morning, a net took my eye and I examined the consignment. It was loaded – a great plunder to be had. I met with some mates at school and the plan was hatched. Summers night at 10.30 with two plastic VG bags in pocket and a plundering we shall go! We had a very agile guy called Andy (who would be a rugby colleague later on in life). He was one of the quickest and wittiest guys I knew. He was small enough to fit under the net and had good hands (he could pick strawberries really fast). There he was, bags in hand and filling them up and handing them to Kevin, who in turn handed them to me (on the wall), and then I to my cousin Barry (over the wall). It was a nice little production line we had going. We had just filled the first VG bag, when the mannies light came on. As I had the highest point, I was the lookout, I shouted, "Here's the mannie!" We all bombed it over the wall, but where was Andy? We saw a torch light reflecting and the mannie shouting fa's there? For sure Andy would be caught, so we waited. The mannie piped up again, "Is there anybody there?" Then Andy, being Andy, said, "Only us strawberries." What could you say or do to that?

The mannie himself must have had a chuckle. He was told to leave the garden. Just as well he never checked the strawberry patch, as a huge chunk of it was in the VG bag, over the wall.

Rumbling the Spoot

The old clay drainpipes see their fair share of rain in Scotland. You certainly got your money's worth with the rain that falls throughout the year. In the summer, during a dry spell (2 full days), we would go out and 'rumble the spoots' which consisted of sticking some newspapers up the drainpipes and setting fire to them, then as the temperature increased, watching as the pipe began to shake and eventually exploded. No use trying this these days, as the pipes are plastic and would just melt. One evening we decided to rumble the old history teacher's house. This guy was a mystery. He lived alone in this seven-bedroom house. We visited the house a lot when we were kids, as he would give us a good chase. The day we rumbled his spout was a double whammy, we set fire to the drainpipe as well as knocked on his door and left a flaming paper bag full of dog shit on his front step. As the pipe began to rumble, the paper was lit he came running out of his house only to be met with a wall of flames, about knee high. He started jumping up and down putting out the flames with every jump. Pretty soon his landing became softer. Couldn't think of anything worse than your slippers smelling of dog shit.

Table Tennis

When you play a sport, you play it with passion and believe that one day you will excel at it. So practice, practice, practice. Table tennis or ping pong (god only knows who called it ping pong) was an excellent sport for hand eye coordination. Most kids these days only get this from switching on and off their Xbox or PS3. My cousin and I were pretty much addicted to the sport, it was true. I was the spin and speed merchant, he was very much the Federer: calm, collected, and ready to kill you off in an instant. The table tennis teacher was also the art teacher at the school (should have been a private investigator). He also was the tennis coach. One Wednesday evening after the school summer holidays, my cousin and me walked up to school to the table tennis club. We started walking on either side of the street, hitting the ball across to each other. I smacked it right over Barry and into a garden full of potatoes. If I was on that side of the street, it would have never happened, as I was the speed merchant remember? So I had to go into the garden as that's the rule knock it in pick it out. I climbed over the wall and, as I was stepping through the guy's tatties, I heard a knock on the window and a shout, "Get the hell out of my garden!" As I climbed back over the wall, ball in hand; I cheekily gestured something to the guy, trundled up to play some Ping-Pong.

The next week at the club, we were asked to line up before we had even done our warm up. We thought we were getting selected for the upcoming tournament and we began muttering to ourselves. As I look across the line, Mr. Farquarson (table tennis/art/PI) was checking shoes and his assistant; the teacher's pet was holding something! When he got to me he said, "Alright whitey, show me your sole." Still curious as to what was happening, the TP, specky twat, said, "It's a match." I said, "No it's not, it's my training shoe, bright spark." The art teacher/PI only went and produced a plaster mold of my training shoe. Bloody hell! I had been rumbled. I was asked to leave the club and wasn't allowed back, I found out the old guy had exaggerated the story and said I dug up half his tatties with my shoes and gave him so much hassle. Oh well, guess who's spout got rumbled later on that week?

Chorrie

I think every child was dared to steal something from the local school shop that everyone visited at lunchtimes, usually by an older friend, a bit like an initiation test. I remember the day I was dared to steal something. I stole a chumpa chump lollipop and put it down my trousers, walked around the store and bought something. As I was paying the cashier, he said, "What about the other item you have?" Of course, I pleaded innocent and as I stood there and pulled out my pockets, she quickly put her hands down my trousers and pulled out the lollipop. It would've been funnier if she had pulled out a cucumber, ha ha. I don't think I had ever been so embarrassed. She called my registration teacher and we were paraded in front of the class and had to apologize to the shopkeeper. I asked them please not to tell my mother. I was more frightened of the retribution from her, than the punishment I would receive from school. My choring school days were over, I didn't have the bottle to do it again. We left it to the professionals, of which there were a few. I had a friend who we used to get to fill half his paper bag and we would share the booty amongst a few friends. Definitely had more balls than myself.

Milky

One of the most sought after jobs when I was growing up was a milk delivery boy, especially working for a certain local firm. One of our friends worked for a particular Dairy and if I calculate how much money he skimmed from them in today's terms, it would be close to 2000 GBP in the two years he was working there. We sometimes would help him in the mornings with the delivery and then on collection days – Friday and Saturday. That was when the real money was to be made. The money was paid weekly and he would put some paid down on the book and some not, he was paying me 20 GBP a week just to hang around with him and be his friend. He didn't need to pay me, but the money was good and I could buy myself some new things and save a little for a rainy day. I remember on one occasion he went to a huge industrial market and spent hundreds of pounds. We went round to his house and he asked me what I liked. I pointed out a leather biker jacket, which he in turn told me he didn't really like… but I could buy it from him for 80GBP (half price). How would I be able to afford it? I quickly thought on my feet and said, "I tell you what, don't give me money for four week's and that would be us quits." He agreed and still gave me the 20 GBP a week, so it was a win win for me. He had a friend keep his extra cash for him under his bed, and at one stage he had 2000 GBP — an unbelievable amount of money in those days. The days of the stealing from the milkie were numbered, though. The sons of the two old guys who ran the business realized there was something wrong when figures weren't quite adding up and pretty soon he was rumbled. The police were involved. To give my friend his due, he didn't try to get us involved and never blamed us, he took all the blame himself. I have a lot of respect for people like that and would do the same myself. Don't bring others down with you. The police definitely wanted more names, but he stood his ground. He moved away from the area but his family stayed. Eventually he joined the Navy, saw the world, and 25 years later moved back home, where he still is today. Nice guy and a heart of gold.

Ice Lolly

Growing up in a small town came with its fair share of boredom, so as kids we had to select friends that we could have a laugh with, take the piss of, and on the odd occasion – fight! I remember on one occasion my cousin and me had been stealing apples at the back of the police station, probably not the most sensible thing to do. As usual, I was the lookout and he was the climber. It wasn't the average apple chorie. He climbed up the wall, with a 'fab' (ice lolly) in one hand and picked apples from the tree with the other. As I sat down to enjoy my fab, I sat on a wasps nest. They were swarming everywhere. I guess I would've done the same if some fat arse sat on my home! I was stung on the ass and leg, and I remember my cousin screaming as the wasps headed towards him. I yelled at him to throw away his fab. He jumped down from the wall, lolly in one hand, while the wasps were stinging him. I ran away up the road to my house, as I went through the door I said to my mum, "I left Barry, he was getting stung with the wasps." She replied, "Where? You better go back, no way there are hundreds of them." We later got a phone call from his mum, saying he was stung unconscious and was in hospital. I went to see him that evening and he had been stung 22 times and someone had picked him up and carried him to the hospital. I was more interested in all the sweets and fruit he had at the side of his bed. I asked him where he had got all that from, and he replied the other patients in the ward had given them. I asked him for some but he said, "No way. If you hadn't ran away, I would have given you some, though."

We were becoming infamous in the town and we were being called the pranksters, it was at this time I started to become friendly with a guy called Stu. Well, it didn't start in a friendly manner, I had a fight with him which in turn lead to another fight or challenge with his older brother. His brother declined and I guess that was where I got some kind of respect from Stu.

We were each other's wingmen; wherever he went, I went and vice versa. He was working for the council as an apprentice joiner, where he finished his trade. Some people said he couldn't join hands, but that's another story.
We began a group in the town, the break-dancers. I wasn't much of a dancer, so I carried the beat box, which required 12 batteries and would generally last only about 12 hours. There was no Duracell in those days. The other guys were,

Sedaka, Josie, Mark, and Stu. We would dance all the time, or, while they were dancing, I was romancing – organizing dates and telling most of the girls I was their manager. We used to go to different towns and roll out the lino (a shiny, slippery carpet) and the guys would body pop, spin on their heads, or perform robotics. When we arrived in the towns the girls would pop down to see us perform and the guys would usually appear for a scrap. I wasn't a dancer, but I sure was a scrapper. I wasn't scared to throw a punch or receive one. I remember one time we took a bus to another town to somebody's leaving party. There were twelve of us. We were running the dance floor and the locals were starting to get wound up. Finally the DJ asked if the Banff boys could please leave as their bus was waiting in the car park. I said, "It's only 11.30, we have 30 minutes to go. The doormen made an escorted line for us, along with the chicks, as we were leaving. I noticed a few notables – guys looking for trouble – peel off. I warned the boys and told them we should go for some fish and chips and see if they were brave enough to follow. I was first out of the chip shop and on the bus. I remember seeing this guy jump on big Gordon Stewart's back. *Wrong move.* He furrled the boy round and gave him a swift kick on the head. Then this other guy came from nowhere and started on Simon. He was a neighbor of mine and definitely wasn't a fighter. They were rolling about the ground and Gordon kicked Simon on the head. It was like something out of the keystone cops. It was about then that I knew my services weren't required and I stayed on the bus and laughed at them as they came back on. The driver was panicking about his bus and was driving off. We had still a few guys left. Stuart and Mark were busy with their silver tongues in the chip shop. I asked the driver to turn back, but he said no way. I went ballistic. There was no way we would leave anybody behind. He said he didn't want his bus wrecked I looked him dead in the eyes, meeting his gaze in the rearview mirror, and said, "We will wreck the bus if you don't turn back." In the end, the driver had very little options.

We often arranged bus trips to other towns; it was a great way to break the mundane life in our small seaside town.

Chapter 4

Senior rugby Tours

I was playing for the under 18 colts, which was a feeder team for our senior club. George ran this club, so I felt entitled to play for it. It was after the game while I was in the changing rooms when George came to me and asked, "How are you feeling?" Then he said, "Fancy a game for the firsts this afternoon? They are short of a player on the wing."

I said yes, of course. I didn't want to say no or that I was shit scared. I went home and told my mum and tried to rest for a few hours, before returning to the grounds. George introduced me to the team. Although I knew their faces, I wasn't familiar with their humor. Big Calvert Mac (local vet) ex SAS guy took me to the side and said, "I will look after you, no need to worry son." That was reassuring. It was the kind of rapport rugby players has, a certain camaraderie that footballers didn't quite have. We were playing a local side that had a great open side flanker and a prop that was an animal. The first 15 minutes of the game were tentative and I was hoping the ball wouldn't come to me. When it did, I ran a little, kicked, and chased it; the more I did this the more I thought, *I could run past half of these guys*. The game was close, it was 4-4 (you used to get 4 points for a try) at half time, our fly half had missed three kicks and was coping some flak at HT in the changing rooms. I said to George who was captain, "Why don't I try the next one." He said, "Don't be too sure, as it's not the same as kicking for the colts."

Ten minutes into the second half, the opposition scored a converted try. They were leading 10-4, and it was then I decided that if I were to receive the ball I would run it. The opposition fly half drilled a ball towards the corner of our 22-meter line. I caught it I could hear the coach telling me to kick it back, but I had other ideas. I ran up the wing and I was one v one with their fullback. I chipped it over his head and the bounce was good, I was in at the corner. I was buzzing, tried to compose myself for the kick, but missed it, 10-8. The time was running down, I received the ball again and got tackled in midfield by the flanker who punched me as I tried to get up. I was seeing stars and then the prop stood on my face and chipped my tooth; game over for me. I was helped to the touchline and asked if I wanted to play on or stay off. We had a penalty, a chance for a kick. It was a different kind of adrenalin, kind of hate towards these two cowards who tried to end my game. I said, "I'm on and I want to take the kick." I slotted it right between the posts and ran towards these two and stuck my fingers up, never speaking a word. The final score was 11-10 and I was the local hero, the feeling was great and the changing room was buzzing. It was then I found out what a man of the match had to do: skull beer and get drunk. My mother was going to kill me. The newspaper clipping calmed her down, though. She was proud of her son, she kept every clipping after that and made a scrapbook. Everyone that came to the house was shown those clippings.

Playing Rugby and having a laugh go hand in hand. There were many characters on and off the field, watching, playing, and socializing after the game. Two particular characters were an elderly couple, Tony and Stella. They had moved into the area and started attending games and volunteered for fundraising activities. Frightfully posh, they were.

Tony had some funny stories to tell, one in particular involved the famous 'Erica Roe'. Anyone who knows anything about Rugby will remember her as the famous streaker with the big breasts running onto the field at 'twickers'. When she jumped back over the barrier, after her famous run, she landed right on Tony's lap. He said, "I didn't know where to look." He stated Stella's boobs were just as big.

I also recalled a time around Christmas where we had an away game in another town called Elgin, after the game there was a kid's party. I took two balloons and stuffed them up my jumper and started to rub them up against Tony saying I was Stella. He was not amused, but I kept doing it until he said I was a disgrace to the club and should never play for the club again. On the way back in the bus he kept on and on about it. When we arrived back at the "Market Arms", he was leaving the bus and tripped and fell and knocked himself out. Too much drink. We helped him into the bar and then ordered him a taxi home. I went round to see if he was ok the next day and said sorry for my actions.

One of the most memorable stories was in a mini bus driving back from England v Scotland. The bus broke down and we were pushing it into the hard shoulder. We were all still half cut, apart from the driver, of course, when our president, Sandy Cassie, slipped. Somehow we managed to push the bus over his legs. We heard an almighty scream. Sandy was lying on the ground with two tire marks across his cream chinos, writhing in agony. Tony piped up and said, "God sake Sandy, looks like you are going to have to change your slacks." Poor Sandy had broken his leg in two places, probably never felt much as it was certainly numbed by the whisky.

Going on tour was the highlight of the season. The Irish and Welsh tours were a month apart and happened every two years. It was a chance to play pranks and have a laugh. The Welsh tour was always first and usually involved a long, 12 hour bus trip. We had a couple of pickups, Turriff, Aberdeen, and Edinburgh and it usually involved drinking games before we got there. We picked up Barney from Turriff. Barney was a farmer who went to a public school, a likeable rogue. He was a whisky drinker; lager or beer didn't agree with him. Nor did whisky, as a matter of fact. We were playing drink while you think on the bus and if you have ever played that game, then you know how it goes. We were approaching Edinburgh and Barney had already drunk 3/4 a bottle of Grouse. He was adamant in coming into the bar, so we propped him up against a pillar just beside a table of old guys. I heard a almighty bang, Barney had fell and knocked the table over spilling the contents of their half deckers and chasers. The old guy nearest to Barney jumped up as if he had been stung in the ass by a bee, he then proceeded to kick Barney in the head. When I look back it seemed such a violent act, but it was really quiet funny and a great way to start the tour. (we diffused the situation by buying the guys more drinks)

We had driven 12 hours and arrived at our destination, St. Athens Bridgend, a disused army barracks. Well done, Bob. He had done it again, top class accommodation in a good rural setting. Had he got somewhere in town, the taxi would have been a lot cheaper.

We had about four hours of sleep before we played against Bridgend athletic, a rugby club who was serious on doing some damage against the weary, traveling scots. We looked like the same group of fearless souls that marched on the fields of Culloden.

The first 5 minutes there was a breakdown in play and we were awarded a scrum, our front row went down and they all received bloodied noses. As they set up again, and we won the strike, I received the ball from the scrum half and drop kicked the ball between the posts for 3 points. Banff 3 - Bridgend Athletic 0. The game ended 86-3. Welcome to Welsh Rugby.

After the game we were playing the usual drinking games, boat race around the broomstick, scull a half pint, spin round the broomstick 10 times, skull another half pint, and run 10 meters or try and run. The guy I went against slipped and fell. I heard a crack and we weren't even in Ireland, forget that different craic. His fellow players rushed over. I thought it was in sympathy, but then they shouted, "Get up, we're going to lose the boat race!" And they did. At least we had one victory that day against the Welsh.

There was one player in particular who stood out. His first name was Robert, last name possibly Jones, Evans, or Williams. Either way, he was a fast motherfucker. I was a 12 second 100m runner. He must have been at least 11. He scored 5 tries that day. He took us out to see the Hotspots of Wales, Bridgend. Some of the team went back to the barracks, but I decided to stay out with my cousin, Barry, and a few others. Robert said, "Let's go back to my place. I will give you guys some beer and more drink and you can try my whisky." We got home and there was a children's play slide. Robert was in the kitchen, trying to serve drinks. I climbed onto the slide, Barry pushed me over, and I landed on the coffee table, which was demolished. The slide was still sticking out of my arse. Robert and the other guys came running through, wondering what the fuck had happened. Then his wife shouted from the top of the stairs. "Robert, I suggest the party is over." We left the party with a few bottles of beer and his finest Scotch. We arrived back to the barracks, me and Barry still looking for mischief. We rolled out the fire hose. The first door we kicked in was Bob's, we shouted, "Fire, fire!" and proceeded to turn the hose on Bob and his bed, soaking him. Next was the bus driver. He was a moody fucker. He wanted to fight, but the power of the hose was enough to push him back to his bed. I thought two reet teets were enough with the hose or there were bound to be repercussions. I heard a few guys outside my room early in morning. I think I got to my bed about two hours before, then door was kicked in, my bed was tipped up with me under it, and the wardrobe was put on top of my bed. The words mentioned were "Make your own way to Cardiff." I guess the bus driver had some say in that.

As I moved all the furniture from my body and made my way to the shower, naked, I heard Barry laughing outside the shower and then a scream. One of the cleaners thought the bus had left along with all the players. I guess she would have put two and two together when she saw the state of the rooms.

We did make it to Cardiff and apologized to the bus driver and Bob. By the way, Scotland did win that weekend in Cardiff, so everyone went home happy.

Jamie was another great character from rugby; he was a rough around the edges sheep farmer, with a great sense of humor. I remember the team going into Aberdeen for a player's fancy dress party. We arranged to pick Jamie and Barney, up just outside Turriff. We had just arrived and these guys were pissing themselves laughing as they got onto the bus. They couldn't wait to tell their story. This is how it went: Whilst waiting for our bus, another bus had come along and it was full of old age pensioners going on a bus run. The two of them had jumped in front of the bus dressed as cowboys with their guns pointed at the driver. The whole bus must have wondered what the hell was going on. I am sure some of the pensioners needed to change their underwear as well. When Jamie and Barney realized it wasn't our bus, they were so apologetic.

On another occasion, we had been playing up in Cathiness and on the Sunday before heading home, we had been invited up to this posh hotel for lunch. As we sat waiting in the dining room for our starters, I happened to look out to the field and saw a flock of sheep. I said to Jamie, looks like your girlfriends are here. The hotel was filling up with families and it wasn't prepared for what was about to happen. Jamie went out and brought a sheep into the dining area and let it go. It ran around, knocking a few kids and tables down before Jamie tackled it and wrestled it to the ground. We never did get those starters. We thought it better we leave these traumatized guests.

'Young's Hotel Edinburgh' was a great venue for Rugby teams, well only for drinking and touring. The bar could accommodate ten people max and was ran by a Chinese family, which doubled as a 24 hour restaurant.

We were sharing the accommodation with Dyce, another crazy Rugby team full of characters: Big Shep, Ally Noble, and Piro Pete. I was sharing a room with George (a good friend and a tour virgin) Sandy, Pookie, and another guy from Dyce, can't remember his name. It was Friday night and we had a few drinks, taking it easy before the game the next day. I suggested to George that we go back to the room and set a few boobie traps. We went to the room. I had the double bed and theirs were two singles and one camp bed. We took the wardrobe down, opened the doors put the fitted sheet over the open doors and lay the pillow on top to make it look like a nicely folded bed. The camp bed was set like a crocodile, it would fold the minute someone put weight on it and would devour the 95kg man who was about to sit in its jaws. We waited for Sandy and his mate to come back. As they entered the room and switched on the light, I said, "Switch it off I can't see." Sandy said, "Fuck sake, Ron, I'm only looking to see were the crocodile is, I mean bed." It was like a simultaneous trap. A shout of, "For fucksake fit the fuck!" Sandy fell into the wardrobe, doors closed and his mate was devoured by the 'croc camp bed'. I shouted, "Put on the light, George." He fell out of the bed laughing. Its times like this you wish there were camera phones and videos around. Fun and priceless, that shit.

If I look back at the things I did and said, I wouldn't change anything. The rugby years and tours were excellent.

Dyce RFC was the only other team that shared Banff's humor as a touring team; they had a great character called Piro Pete. I remember during an Irish tour we had been staying in this guesthouse that was ran by a father and his five daughters (catholic). They were like the Gestapo, if you thought you would sneak a girl back to your room, you had more of a chance of Scotland winning the world cup.

We had arrived at the hostel in our usual drunken stupor, 20 males looking for fun, women, and watching rugby. And, of course, Guinness, the Black Gold. Trust me when I say this is a beer that doesn't travel well, I know, If I can drink 12-16 pints of this, then anyone can. We were sitting in the dining room talking with the girls when I noticed some trays for glasses, dishes, etc. I said to Andy, "Do you fancy taking part in the winter Olympics?" (as this happened to be on TV at the time)

He looked at me, confused but inquisitive. I knew he was up for a giggle. I told him it was winter Olympics, Banff V Dyce, two man bobsleigh and luge. Of course, this had to be practiced on the trays.

Everyone climbed up the five story carpeted staircase. Andy and myself were first. We both made it to the bottom, though I still have carpet burn marks to this day.

Next up was Piro Pete. He decided to go head first, just because he was a lunatic. The first flight, he dived on the tray and he slid down the stairs at a great rate of knots and of coarse he couldn't stop himself and ended putting his head through the plasterboard. Game over, the girls quickly said. They also told us we'd be getting a bill for that. It was well worth it, even though I didn't see it, as we were waiting at the bottom for the medal ceremony.

The next day, Pete was nowhere to be seen. One of the girls said he was up early and had his breakfast and then out he went.

He came back with two boxes of oranges, about 100 in total. He said, ok let's continue Banff V Dyce. We were confused. Why the oranges?

He replied, "Banff on 1 side of the street and Dyce on the other, for every player struck with an orange you are awarded points: head 4 points (try) chest 3 points (drop goal or penalty) leg / arm 2 points (conversation). What a laugh. I don't know what the score was, but there a few startled pedestrians, not to mention the cyclist that took a head shot, luckily he was wearing a Helmet.

We arrived at the horseshoe bar, this was a great drinking venue, next to Lansdowne road, and I was amazed at all the chip vans. There must have been around 50 at either side of the road. After the game, we were walking back and a couple of guys decided to buy some burgers. I said to Andy, "Lets continue with the theme Banff V Dyce. You are one side of the road and me on the other. Let's see how many chip vans' generators we can switch off." It was bloody hilarious and a lot of 'what the fucks' from the owners.

Another great tour character was Big Ally. He was a legend on tour with his squeezebox and his unmistakable fart noises, which he could produce with his hands and lips, a man who could play the legendary Muppet theme tune between his fingers.

We eventually arrived back at the B&B and Radar knob (the name had been changed to protect his character) that famously sat in a bar in Ireland at 9am and got pissed off, as there were no women in the bar and preceded to the bakery next door to ply his charm. You see, for some, tours were a way of getting away from family and letting your hair down and not worrying about your wife giving you shit for coming in all hours of the night.

Later that night as we sat in the B&B, Radar knob came in and looked quite flustered. I said, "The last time I saw you, you were speaking to that group of women, what happened?" He replied, "I always wanted to shag a heavily pregnant chick." We knew he was an animal, but this took it to another level. What had happened, the woman's husband, a burly black guy had returned unexpectedly, Radar Knob feared for his life, jumped out the bedroom window, and ran for his life. Luckily enough, the guy didn't follow, as Radar was somewhat slower than the infrared rays of his signals.

The next day was one of the funniest touring days ever.

Sunday sessions in Dublin were outstanding. 10.30am - 10.30pm drinking black gold and having a giggle, so many things can happen or go wrong!

It was around 3 pm when the females starting streaming into the bar. I guess after mass, it was time to let their hair down. The band already had been playing for an hour, cranking out the Irish folk music. All the guys were kilted up; the last day in our kilts was always a good choice of attire and certainly was an attention grabber.

I was standing at the bar next to a group of girls and avoiding eye contact, looking at them through the mirror behind the bar. I smiled and was met with a returning smile. The smiler approached and said, 'us girls are having a bet and we are wondering if you guys are true Scotsmen' (as if we hadn't heard that before). They suggested I go back and choose five mates to flash their cash and the girls would be a drink to the winner.

I said, "What are the rules?"

They said:

1. Length

2. Girth

I said, "One more." They looked puzzled. I replied, "Presentation."

They agreed and I went back and told the guys the two rules, then I went to the toilet and my plan was hatched.

I picked up a party streamer and wrapped it around my balls and dick. It was like a prize peacock with its feathers blooming. I summoned the troops and off we set for the knob and ball pageant.

As we approached, we could see these girls laughing. They seemed apprehensive, a bit like they were when they lost their virginity or perhaps they hadn't, being good catholic girls. We stood in a line and the girls waited as we all lifted the kilts. They all looked at mine with amazement. It wasn't the size or the girth (not what I say to all the girls) it was the secret question, (presentation) 'party streamer art', at its finest. I had won the bet 10/10 for presentation. The guys were all crying foul, but soon realized I had one over again, a pint of the black gold. I said.

As the afternoon grew old and the band struck up their reportage of the commitments (a movie as famous as the full Monty), Ireland's answer to 'Braveheart' there was a song and the lyrics went 'too many fish in the sea.'

When the song came on, I asked the barmaid for scissors and cut two fish shapes out of an old newspaper, one for Pookie and myself. I gave one to him and we went over beside the fish tank. We started to wriggle the fish outside the tank and the whole bar was pissing themselves laughing. It was the sort of spontaneous thing I would come up with, anything for a laugh. Talking about spontaneous, Guinness and farts are synonymous, where there's Guinness, the beer farts are incredible. We returned to our seats and Pookie would have one last party piece, if he didn't win the bet for the penis show, he would earn a few beers as he lifted his kilt and lit a beer fart. Any bloke who has done this will see the humor behind it; it's a bit like chicks laughing at friends. Pookie had saved the best fart till last. He let out a belter as he held the naked flame next to his ring, (Was there not a famous Johnnie cash song ring of fire? Do you think this came from lighting farts? Not sure if JC would have done this.) A blue flame shot out of his arse like a rabbit from a burrow. Pookie singed his jeer and the whole bar erupted again, who are these crazy scots. He spent the next half hour in the toilet, ass under the cold water tap cooling his ring.

These are memories that I will never tire of talking about and hearing, even writing this now, I am laughing my head off.

Shetland 7's.

We caught the PO regular ferry from Aberdeen to Shetland on Thursday at 8 o'clock and arrived at 8am the next day. The trip was always eventful, usually 3 or 4 teams making the trip along with a couple of women's hockey teams, as they had a tourney in Bressie (small island east of Shetland) on Sunday, during which the Rugby guys would go across on the small ferry and eye up the talent.

Whilst on the ferry, I spotted a guy approaching the bar with his girlfriend/wife he looked the double of Lemmy from Motorhead (ace of spades). Me and Ally both looked at each other. Ally farted out the Ace of spades with his hands while I sang the lyrics. The whole Place was pissing with laughter and the poor guy had one drink and as he left, I shouted, "Don't forget the joker!" the banter was flowing, insults between the teams were heating up and as each guy left, the banter grew louder. Unbeknown to us, sitting in the corner was the Great White Shark (not the golfer) but John Jeffery, he happened to be there with his wife. He came across and sat beside us, the whole 6 ft 8 of him. He said, "Guys, I have been on British Lions tours, Scottish tours, and haven't seen anything as crazy as you lot, bloody hilarious. Andy stood up and pulled a tape measure from his pocket, he was famous for taking props, as you never knew when you needed one. The last time he used the tape measure was in Ireland when a couple of drug dealers (dope kind) had crashed their car into a tree. They were refusing to open the doors and the Garda were getting more and more annoyed. Andy pulled out the tape measure and measured the skid marks on the road and said to the cops, "Ha ha they got bigger skid marks than you." The guys were rolling in their car. I guess five minutes before it was a joint that was being rolled; now it was laughter.

You canna beat a giggle. So many stories I could write a book. Oh wait a minute, I 'am.

Getting back to the Great White. As Andy produced his tape measure, he asked JJ to stand up. Andy was around 5ft 6 he had to stand on a stool to measure him and as he measured across his shoulders, he told him to turn up next week at training and he might get a game for the seconds. Again the hilarity was there. As JJ left, Andy shouted, "If you run out of breath, knock on my cabin. I will come and finish the wife off!" Only he could get away with saying that.

Saturday before the tourney was always a relaxed affair, a little bit of shopping, mixing with the locals, and a good giggle. We went past this hardware shop, I looked in the window and saw a chainsaw. I looked at Ally and said deek deek. He knew exactly what was going to happen. Ally, Pookie, and myself went into the shop. I went to the counter and a young assistant approached me. Ally and Pookie headed in the direction of the chainsaws. I said to the guy, I want to buy some paint, as we need to paint the lines for the Rugby this afternoon. The guy told me he didn't think that was the type of paint you used. Of course, I knew, it just gave Ally and Pookie more time. All I heard was what sounded like a chainsaw starting and Pookie running towards the young assistant with the saw. All I could see was the look of terror, which was quickly defused by my laughter, the young guy realized it was a joke and joined in with the laughter. You need a laugh from time to time and I think we have had a good share of laughs along the years.

On Sunday, we boarded the ferry to Bressie. It was a 10-minute crossing. You could throw a stone between the two isles. Big Sheppy decided he wanted to go up to the bridge and speak to the captain. It was about 12 feet up to the captain's bridge. Shep must have asked him if he could go out beside the rails because when he came out, he shouted, "Bar dive!" We assumed the catch position. For those who don't know what a bar dive is, this is a dive generally from no higher than 6ft for safety reasons and you must have trust in your mates to catch you. Sheppy was performing this from much higher and he was around 100kg. As we secured or links, he dived. He misjudged the distance and he folded like a green final, his head bouncing off the metal flooring. With blood pissing from his head, we thought he was dead. Of course he was unconscious and the ferry turned around and we took him to the hospital. We arrived back at Bressie just in time for the final. Andy decided to run onto the field naked. Well, with one red sock on, as they were doing the coin toss. The ref was none too happy. She muttered something to Andy. She only asked me to put my other sock on, Andy forever the joker, later said.

On the way back in the ferry, the captain seemed concerned for him. He was required to stay in the hospital for observation until he fully recovered. We found out the following week we had been banned from the 7's tournament, simply because of the naked hockey event and the ferry bridge dive. We went up a couple of years later and played under Dyce. As we went across on the Bressie ferry, the captain recognized me and said, "Do you know every day we talk about that dive and still can't believe he did it and survived?"

It wasn't to be the last ferry our club would be banned from.

The club's 25th anniversary was a trip to Holland. 30 players and supporters attended the trip. As we boarded the ferry from Hull to Zeebruger, we noticed a few hen parties and knew the crossing would be fun.

As a group checked around the ferry, we were quite impressed; night club, casino, food area, and a shopping area. I think if a woman were writing this book, the order would be slightly different. We quickly dumped the bags in the cabin and headed straight to the bar. We watched it gradually fill up and, as the atmosphere heated up, the boys were getting more and more boisterous. We were getting well into the celebrations, when we noticed a Hen party come through the door and the guys latched on. I had the more subtle approach: assess and wait for the perfect opportunity. The problem with most guys is they assess the situation and then end up getting too drunk and the girls go home frustrated. There is always a song that fills the dance floor, doesn't matter what generation you grew up, 'Paradise by the dash board light' 'New Years day' U2, you name it it fills the floor. The floor filler during this rugby tour was The Full Monty, the song was made famous by a film made in Sheffield about a group of guys trying to raise money for there local community center. It so happened the Hen Party were all from Sheffield, when they played the song about 5 guys from our club got up and about 10 of the girls from the Hen party, as the song goes along people are supposed to take there clothes off and leave everything but your hat on. Of course neither of us or the girls in that case had hats, so it was a case of calling each others bluff, most guys stopped at there boxers, but hey ho not me, along with a couple of others we were naked, everyone started shouting off off off, hoping the girls would get naked also. To everyone's pleasant surprise two blonde girls, very nice I may add, removed all of their clothes, the bar went wild everyone was cheering and clapping, I picked a girl up and put her on my shoulders so everyone could see, that was a great night and an excellent way to start the tour.

I find the Dutch very boring and seem to have a small sense of humor. They are loud and can be wound up easily. You could see our behavior off the field was annoying them also. We decided it was time to leave, as we left in a group, a great mix of experienced players, new ones, and non-players. First stop was the 'banana bar' and we all sat in the front row. A couple of guys volunteered for the stage, Pookie and George. Pookie was first; he wasn't being cooperative at all. He ended up making a tail out of toilet paper, stuck it between his butt cheeks, set fire to it, and rushed around stage. This was the dance of the fiery assholes.

Then it was George's turn. He was up for anything. As he lay on the floor, semi-naked with his boxers on, the girl approached him. She had handcuffs in one hand, shaving foam and a banana in the other. George freely let the girl handcuff him; she then sat him down and put the banana in his mouth. She was gyrating her ass around his face and then she covered him with shaving foam.

I saw his clothes at the corner of the stage, so I took them and ran outside and put them inside a wheelie bin.

He stuck his head outside the door and shouted at me to give his clothes back, calling me a prick. Eventually, I gave them back and the famous words were mumbled, "I'll get you back for that."

When the tour was over as we boarded the ship back home we were met by the captain, he said I have warned the DJ not to play that song again, so no one will be getting naked on my ship again. We were reasonably well behaved on the trip back, but we still received a letter from PO Ferries, we were banned from that particular route.

Chapter 5

Growing up amongst Banff Legends

Black Hughie and Family

There are many local heroes in my hometown of Banff and this particular family I'm about to tell you about were in that category. Bouquie, Parrot, Black Hughie, and his wife Nellie.

You would often see B and P pushing a pram filled with sticks from the fir widies (a small gathering of fir trees at the top of Banff). They would venture up there nearly every day and gather firewood to light their fire with. You see, Black Hughie (the father) worked at the Robertson's coal shed. He filled the bags with coal. I think he filled his piece bag also, because his lumb was always reeking!

One day, Barry and myself borrowed my brother James' handheld CB radio and walked down through the town, we approached Black Hughie's house, we heard Parrot saying his handle, "pot black". It was taken from his snooker hero, John Parrot. I am guessing the nearest parrot had been to a snooker cue, was deeking at a pool cue at Ma Black's.

I took the handheld CB and said, "Breaker on the side, breaker on the side." Pot black replied, "Come in." That was a cue to for me say something. I said, "It's mad Mac here!" That was the owner of a local taxi firm, where he would run the social scroungers around town, especially on their giro day! You see, black Mac was the only bread winner in the family and basically he worked himself to death, to support his family, while his two sons went collecting sticks during the day and drinking Friday, Saturday, and Sunday, all they lived on was there social security giro. The first thing I said while on the CB Radio, was their mother was barred from getting in my taxi forever. He asked me what for and I said, "The last time she was in the taxi she pissed all over the back seat. There is a afa hum oh piss and I can't get rid of it!" I heard the whole family going berserk, shouting and screaming that they were coming to my door to sort it out! I told them to come ahead. Barry and me went into the phone box next to their house, pretending to make a call, Back Mac, Bouquie, and Parrot marched past going crazy. We waited a couple of minutes and followed suit. They stopped in past Ma Black's, for a half decker and a chaser and guess who paid? Yes you guessed – the coal winner. Mac's taxis was a stone's throw away from Ma Black's, but they must have told the whole three customers in the bar what they were about to do. There was another character in there, Ian Mac. I have another story about him as well. Out the three amigos came and headed towards Mac's door. Bang, bang, bang! It wasn't a gun; it was Parrot giving the door a fair drilling. Mac came to the door and the three amigos stepped back. Mac said, "What the fuck are you doing wrapping at my door at this time of night?" The three amigos looked more confused than a drifter (a famous chocolate sweetie at the time). Bouquie stepped forward, being the biggest, but probably the daftest hard man in Banff at the time, he said, "You said my mother pissed in your car and you can't get rid of the smell!" Mac replied, "There's many a time she comes in the car reeking of strang, but I have a peg. I just put that on my beak and I cannot smell the strang." Well, Bouquie flashed (when someone gets so angry, they react in a violent manner). He threw a punch from the canalers to the cemetery, about the length of Banff. Stevie Wonder would have seen it coming. Sandy Mac moved and Bouquie fell right inside the house. What a miss, hadn't seen one as bad since Tore Andre Flo missed that goal under the bar against Celtic. Giving Sandy his due, I think most people would have booted him in the heed. I ken, Soles would have (not a bad football player). Sandy just allowed him to stand up and then he closed the door and that was that, the three amigos walked back up the road.

Fingers

Fingers was another character and neighbour. He was a kind-hearted gentleman (when sober) that was harmless and known in the community. I lived most of my life at 16 Malcolm road, at number 20, Fingers stayed with his sister, Sandra. He was a whisky drinking, likable character, who had a great talent of playing the spoons. We used to ask him on a regular basis to crank out a tune. He was good fun and you would always see him at Ma Black's through the window with the spoons in his hand, never a good singer but had an ear for music. On the odd occasion he would come home drunk and find himself locked out. I had returned from the U18 disco, with my mate Robbie one night and saw Fingers knocking on the door, shouting, "Sandra let me in!"

Robbie and myself had a plan before that. We had been to the local chip shop and stole a few tomato sauce sachets. We planned to knock on my door and my sister would answer and Robbie would have this sauce spread all over his face and be collapsed on the doorstep. I, of course, was hiding!

It worked perfect. My sisters were shouting, "Where's Ron?" Robbie was a great actor; I managed to hold my laugh for about 30 seconds before I stepped from behind the doorstep.

As we went into the house, I asked them why they were still awake. They said Fingers had been shouting for almost an hour and they couldn't get to sleep. We filled a bucket of water, crept up on him, and I said, "Ok, the door is open." As he moved towards Sandra's door, we threw the water all over him, he stood there liked a drookit rat, his face was priceless. When I look back on some of the things I did, I cringe, but in my eyes it was harmless fun.

Cakie Burnett

Another great character of Banff, lived in the middle of the Gallowhill (a place where the famous sheep rustler Macpherson was hung). I didn't think he supported Aberdeen, so he just chored the sheep and did nothing else with them.

Barry and I were at the youth club, a place where you could go twice a week, walk down the road and walk home and not worry about getting into any trouble. Well, it depends how far you went afterwards! We used to visit the crown hotel, where Dod Adams would allow us to go upstairs and play pool. You see, we could have played pool at the youth club, but you had to wait so long for a game and the older kids seemed to hug the table (that's not cuddling it, that's crowding it, so you couldn't get on). So we used to have a few games at the Crown. As we were leaving, I saw this cleaner's cabinet and thought I would have a look inside. I saw this cleaning fluid inside a dispenser and decided to acquire it, just then Cakie was leaving the bar after a few jars. He was such a menace in the bars; he was banned from every other one in Banff, not for fighting but for sneaking behind the bar and pouring himself a drink! He said, "What are you trying to hide from me?" I said, "It's McEwen's export and we are squirting it in our mouths to get drunk." (I knew this was his favorite tipple). I knew what the next question would be, as I held it in front so he could deek at it. He said, "Geese a drink oh at!" I told him no way, it was for us. Barry told me to give him a drink, just to egg him on. I said, "Ok Cakie, open your mouth." And I squirted it right at the back of his throat. As his taste buds began to react, behind the taste oh woodbines and stale beer, he began to cough and splutter. He shouted, "You wee bastard!" and proceeded to chase Barry and me. For those who know Banff, he chased us to the Royal Oak, to the top of the Gallowhill. It was the biggest chase in history). In distance terms, it was about, 1k and it was mostly all uphill. As we reached the top of the hill, we saw Cakie stop, I was so happy he finally stopped. He must have slept for a few days after.

Stan and Biffo

A great double act was Stan and Biffo, one famous story that circulated the town of Banff. I will tell you two, as I witnessed one, so I know that this was true.. The first story involved Cakie. Stan and Biffo went everywhere together. I would have liked to hear what they were talking about scheming. One famous story was that the famous Sherriff Crone sentenced Stan to 30 days in prison. Stan replied, "I will do that standing on my head." Sherriff Crone replied,

"Then you can do another 30 days standing on your feet. 60 days Mr. Clark" Classic.

Ok, here's story one. It was giro day and the Gallowhill was a hive of activity. Everyone was buzzing about, paying debts, eating scran, and the favorite activity, drinking peeve. Stan and Biffo ventured across to Cakie's gaff and decided to bring their usual carry out, two beers, one each. They knew Cakie would have a supply from Macgregor's shoppie, as Ina (the shop owner) would be stocked up with Cakie's favorite tipples, McEwan's and a bottle of grouse, because he was feeling flush. Because somebody was paying him for the gutted rabbits he would bring back, from the dump or the fir widies. S and B asked Cakie for a chaser (a small whisky) not the kind that he gave my cousin and me a few years before. Cakie obliged and Stan said, "I'll pour it!" You see, Cakie's bunker was fair full of coal, as he also received his monthly allowance. Stan had a plan.

I sort of felt sorry for Cakie, once upon a time he would have been a hard working character, but there was a story going around, his wife and kid went down to Macgregor's shop for a loaf and jam and never came back. They had been away for almost 10 years. I guess they had enough, can't blame them really. But, as a father, it would be quite gut wrenching if that happened to me.

So Stan's plan was about to hatch, he was pouring Cakie doubles and knew on an empty stomach, Cakie would be pissed in no time. The plan was taking shape. You see, Biffo was a painter, so he wandered across to his house and got some black paint. By this time, Cakie was well on his way and was really drunk. His yaks were going together and he was nodding off. The plan was hatched, paint all Cakie's windows black, so when he woke up, he still would think it was dark, giving them time to chore his coal and sell it, you canna make that shit up, quality. Those who knew Cakie, he would just wake up, see it was still dark and take a drink oh whisky and go back to sleep, some folk said he slept for two days. But one thing was for sure, his coal bunker was empty!

Stevie

Steve was a likeable rogue who had a heart of gold. I had known him for a long time. There was one night sitting in our local bar, Seafield on a Thursday night and I was asking him if he had any pets. He replied, "I had a dog called Lucky. Oh I loved that animal." he said. i asked what happened to it. He said it had been run over one day when he was walking it. I asked if it killed and he told me no, but it received a broken leg. "Oh," I replied. "That's kind of ok." He then burst into tears and said six months later it was run down again and killed. I replied it couldn't have been very lucky then. He was crying like a baby.

On the very evening John and me were waiting for Steve to go home, we decided to follow him in John's car. You see, Steve stayed in a flat beside the police station, and this flat had a veranda, which overlooked the sea. He was sitting on the veranda smoking a joint looking out to the sea on this particular summer evening. As we drove past, the plan was hatched. I said to John, "Do you still have that white sheet in the back of your car?"

He replied 'yes I have', and then asked me what I wanted it for.

I replied, "I want to go onto the beach and climb up the ladder and freak the shit out of Steve." As I climbed down the ladder adjacent to the ship inn, I walked across to the ladder facing Steve's veranda. I climbed up and shouted, 'Steeeven Steeeven' in my best ghostly voice. I heard him reply, "Ghosts man ghost man!" I could hardly detain myself from laughing!

The next day, we went into the bar to tell the owner about it and he was pissing himself laughing and said Steve had already been in and told him about the ghost climbing up the ladder.

Muppet

The Seafield front bar on a Thursday night was a place where we could hang out and play pool, very occasionally some girls would come to the bar, especially the student nurses from the local mental hospital. We used to go back sometimes for a party, but more often than not we weren't welcome, as we couldn't be trusted.

One night in the bar, one of the legends of the town came in – Georgie Collier (muppet). He was the hardest man in the town or so he thought. He could talk a good game, but I never once saw him fight; he was a gentle midget.

He had been drinking all day and he was going to venture home, so we decided to follow him. We stood outside the flats across from the town and country club. They had just been renovated, and I found a tin of paint and opened the lid. As Georgie walked past, I shouted from the shadows and threw the paint up in the air and it just landed right on George's head and proceeded to cover his whole body. He walked 20 yards to the central and banged on the door. Baxi (owner, god rest his soul) came down and said, "What the fuck happened to you, man?" John and me walked up and made on we never knew anything about it and asked the same question. Georgie replied, "It was a boy from Macduff, let's go and get him. I'm going to blin him." I replied, "Georgie you are already blind, man, with that paint in your eyes." We all had a laugh, apart from the Muppet.

Chapter 6

The Flat Years

First Flat Mate

John (Pookie) was a quiet guy when he didn't drink, but a total menace when he did. He was probably one of the funniest guys I have ever come across. We had some good laughs together, sober or drunk.

41A Low Street, Banff, will go down in the history books in Banff. It was the summer of 1999 and it was about time I left the comfort of my mother's house. You see, taking a girl back to your mum's house is not cool, especially when you are 35 years old. I had left home once before, but that was when I was 19. I headed into the big city of Aberdeen and started work as a kitchen porter in a famous retail firm. I stayed two years, but I really missed the small town mentality and especially my rugby-playing companions.

The first day I moved into the flat, I saw the potential. It was well situated not too far from the takeaways, fast food heaven. I was never the cook my mother was, but I did try on occasion. As I was sitting on the window ledge looking across the street, watching the world go by and reflecting on how things in my life would pan out, I saw a regular band of people walking in and out of the bus shelter, using the phone box, waiting for calls, staying on the phone for hours. I thought, *we could have lots of fun with this.*

I will always remember that number: 815655. I wonder if I called it today, would it ring and would people still answer it and fall for the pranks? I can't remember the first call I made, but there are so many that sticks in my mind.

The only annoying thing about the flat was during the summer months, there would be young seagulls mating and nesting and having baby chicks. The noise would be quite deafening, this would start around 9 pm-11pm and then 3 am - 8am every firkin morning.

The Bomb

There was a guy in Banff, called Wobbly Willie. The reason people called him that is because he shook a lot when you spoke to him and the more you spoke to him, the more he wobbled. It seems cruel, but he liked people talking to him, as not many people took time to do so! Little did I know, this was going to turn into a double prank. I saw Willie sitting beside the phone box waiting for the bus to take him home. I knew the bus wasn't due to arrive for another 30 minutes. Not only did I know the phone number, I also was familiar the bus timetable. So I dialed the number. Generally, people looked around and wonder what to do, but not Willie. This was an opportunity for him to talk to someone. It rang twice, and then he wobbled over and answered it! I said, "Are you listening carefully?" He replied that he was. I said, "There is a bomb in the bucket outside the pizza shop (Eddie the Egyptian). I want you to go across and tell everyone to get out of the pizza shop, as I will detonate the bomb in 5 minutes." If you could have seen the speed he moved at, it was almost unbelievable. Faster than Usain Bolt from the blocks. Because the pizza shop was only about 50m from my house, I could hear everything Willie said! He ran into the shop and said, "Get out, get out there is a bomb inside the bucket!" Fair play, he got everyone out, as Eddie skeptically inspected the empty bin, he realized it was a false alarm.

He must have felt sorry for Willie in his flustered state and he gave him a pizza. You see, Eddie was a genuine character, whom I had a good relationship with. Well, I put a lot of business his way. He would always give me extra toppings, I suppose that's what business is about: a favor for a favor.

Willie ventured across the street, pizza in hand reflecting on the bomb hoax and looking at the pizza box. What else could happen on this eventful late summer evening? Willie munched away at his pizza, waiting for the last bus, as he had missed the previous one due to his good deed to society. Well, at least he had been awarded with a pizza. If you know Banff, directly opposite 41A was the townhouse, a building where people came for planning permits, paying council tax, and general complaining about the council's lack of response time for their services. It was also a great nesting area for the scourge of any seaside town, the Seagull. The time was fast approaching the sea gulling hour, where they would swoop down looking for food, and of course they would target Willie. I saw one perched on the roof tops about 50ft above Willie, and I thought if I went upstairs and shot it, it would perhaps fall from the roof and land next to him. What were the chances? I remember calling the council and asking them about my seagull problem. I received a shock when the guy said, "Do you have air rifle?" I said told him I didn't, but I was sure I could get one. He replied, "That's how you control them." So they gave me the authority to shoot them, as long as it was after 10pm. So I purchased a high power air rifle, I think my highest kills was 32 in one summer.

So here we go. Picture this Willie tucking into his pizza and sitting peacefully on the bench, minding his own business and now innocently perched 50ft above his head were two seagulls, having a screaming competition. I decided to go upstairs to have a pot shot. My bedroom was an attic room and you can't see the main road (where traffic moved) from my room. I could see the plainsteens and the townhouse and where Willie was sitting. I took my rifle and took aim through the sites, the first slug whistled past the two gulls heads, at a fair rate of knots. Usually this was enough to make the birds fly off, but it proceeded to bring them to a greater chorus. I set my sights and the next shot was bang on target, right on the bird's chest. It fell and lay perched motionless on the roof. For 5 seconds the other bird sat and wondered, "What happened to my mate?" Then all hell broke loose. The bird flew up and started to shit everywhere, I am not sure if any of it landed on Willie or his pizza, I don't know if anyone has killed a seagull, but the reaction after is quite spectacular. They fly around screaming, swooping, and pooping. I decided to retreat to my window seat where I had full view of Willie, still eating his pizza. Out of the corner of my eyes, I saw the gull sliding down the roof. Surely this wasn't going to be a two birds with one stone scenario? The bird was gaining speed and the unsuspecting Willie was about to get the shock of his life, the bird landed on his seat about a foot away from him. Up he jumped, pizza in the air. *Poor fellow*, I thought. He was going to have a heart attack. As the seagulls devoured the remainder of the pizza, Willie retreated to the safer haven of the bus Shelter and waited for his bus. I rang the phone box again, but he was never going to answer, as he had had enough stress for the evening.

The Bobbies (police)

Every second Tuesday, I had a day off and it so happened to be court day. This was a day were the locals who had been in trouble with the law would have to appear in court, as they had done something illegal.

I had a good friend who was training to be a pilot; he also worked with me and was probably one of the few guys that got my sense of humor. I was getting ready to go to work and he called and asked if I wanted to go for lunch. I told him to come across, no problem.

I was getting ready and we were sitting in pole position, looking from the flat window. I mentioned that in 10 minutes the police would be walking past for their lunch break from court proceedings. George asked if I had any yogurt and muesli. I knew what he was scheming, and I replied with an excited, "Yes!" I mixed some up and gave him the bowl and the spoon. The plan was hatched. As mentioned before, we had a very large population of seagulls, living in a coastal town.

I looked out of my window and, as regular as clockwork, the bobbies were walking back towards the station. There were four of them about 20 meters apart. George opened the window and lobbed a lump of yogurt muesli right on top of their police hats. They looked up disgruntled and their colleagues laughed at what had just happened. Little did they know, they were going to get a double dose. Their colleagues received exactly the same as what they had just got.

I suppose that's why George and myself were on the same wavelength.

I met him through another friend of mine, a guy called John (Dopey). He told me of this young apprentice he was working with and he had asked George one day to go and get him some cigs and some cola from the shop. If they haven't got the cigs and cola, he was told to get something else. He came back with an orange and a car magazine. That was my kind of humor.

German Tourists

The thing about staying in the flat was there was always some unsuspecting person willing to answer the phone! Directly below the flat was a newsagent and every Wednesday and Saturday, many locals would purchase a 'national lottery ticket', the one and only chance to become a millionaire in that small northeast town (unless your name was Mr Cheyne).

The last call for the lottery ticket was 7pm. Yes, I bought one every week and never won more than a tenner.

One Saturday evening I was relaxing, just getting ready to go out, when I looked across and saw two German tourists standing next to the bus shelter! Not that I knew they were Germans, they weren't wearing any memorabilia from the beer festival. I called the phone box and I could see them looking at each other in a confused manner! They hesitated and Wolfgang answered the phone (wasn't his name really). He said hello in his best English accent and I spoke slowly so he would understand what I was saying. I said, "Can you help me please, I am trapped!" "Where?" he replied! I said, "Directly opposite where you are standing, across the street inside the newsagents, I am locked in the toilet and can't get out, can you please come across and lift the gate and free me. Please understand am not Jewish!"

The guy told his Frauline and she sheepishly wandered across the street and tried lifting the gate. She obviously wasn't observant enough to see the giant padlock!
She shouted to Wolfgang, "I can't get it up!" He said to me, "I am just going across to help my Frauline. Wait, you will soon be free." I looked from the window and could see them shaking the gate vigorously, but to no avail. Wolfgang came back to the phone and asked, "What should I do?" I told him that perhaps he could go to the local police station, it was about 500m. I gave him directions. It was at this time I asked him where he was from and he replied Munich. I said thank you very much, you are so kind. I said my grandfather was in the concentration camps. There was a silence and then he said, "I have no allegiances to the Nazi party." I said, "No, my grandfather was on the watchtower. He was shooting the Jews when they tried to escape." (Only joking by the way).

They hung the phone up and headed towards the police station, about 10 minutes later the police came around, which was fast for them. They dropped the tourists off and looked up to the flat. They were shaking their heads, another piece of harmless fun. I don't think the tourists wrote about that in their diary.

Dog shit

Pookie and me were out doing the circuit and about to go home when we spotted a friend, Davie, speaking to a girl in another car. He was dropping a few innuendos and it was only a matter of time before they went looking for a park (that was a secluded area where they could get close and intimate). We followed them for a while and then gave up, as I had another idea. You see, before poop scoops and dog litter bags, any town in the UK had its fair share of places where dogs would go to plum, usually the pavement and generally you would find yourself sliding on it!

I said to pookie, let's get some dog shit and put it on the door handle of Davie's car. We will also put some on the passenger door handle, we went and bought some items from the local mini mart and we asked for an extra plastic bag, so we would carry the dogshit in. We drove to the local grounds, where many a time we had stood on it or landed on it. What possesses people to have their dogs crap on the rugby or football pitch, I will never understand. Maybe it's the unsporting members of society. I picked two pieces up with the bag and, as Pookie was driving, I wafted the bag in front of his nose. He was choking as he was driving. I found it amusing, though am sure he never did. As we approached Davie's car, I ran the scenario through in my head, wondering how I would feel if somebody did the same thing to me! To be perfectly honest, I couldn't have cared less if they did the same; a laugh is a laugh in my books. I smeared the dog shit under the door handle of the driver and passenger door, and we waited for Davie to return. When he came back, we called him across to our car and asked him what did he get, which was a term for asking if he get laid or was it just a bit of harmless fun. He replied, "I got a stinky." (That's a term for giving a girl a fingering). I thought, *he is about to get another stinky from the door handle.* As we waited for him to open his car door, he must have thought, *Why are they not driving away!* Two seconds later, as he opened the door and felt this warm, soft, squashy turd, he knew why. He smelled his hand and almost vomited. He drove all the way home with his hand out of the window, no wet wipes in them days. He called me the very next day. Well, in fact, it was his mother who called and said, "I'm going to kill you the next time I see you!" Apparently, Davie drove her to work that morning and exactly the same had happened to her. Double whammy strikes again.

Fishy VW Golf

One friend had called me up to ask me where George was, knowing full well where he was! I told him he was in London doing his flight training for going to work for 'Virgin Atlantic'. My mate said, "Can you ask George a favor? Can you ask him if I can park my car outside his flat? You see the mate in question is renowned for being a tight ass, so this would save him some airport parking fees." I told him to ask him himself.

I briefed George that he would call him to ask. George called me and said, what can we do to his car? I told him there was nothing I could do, as i was 500 miles away. If anything could be done it would be him that did it!

My mate called George and said what he had to say and George said no problem, he can park it there. It had been parked outside his house for two days and George called me and asked if I had any ideas yet. I said I saw in the paper the other day that Gazza put some fish in Gordon Durie's car and he had a problem, obviously, with the smell. George said, "That's it – I will do the same!"

I thought he would wait maybe another 10 days at least, but George never did things on half measures. He went out that very day and put five fish in his Volkswagen golf GTI, my mate's pride and joy. About two days before my mate and his wife were to come back from holidays, I got a call from George saying he was going to New York, and he would be back in four days. I knew the first thing that would happen, my mate would be on the phone asking me what the fuck happened to his car. *Ron do you know anything about this*, he'd ask.

As the very evening arrived, I was lying in my bed and at midnight I received the phone call. His exact words were, "Where the fuck is that bastard? I'm not happy. I have removed five fish from my car and the wife, is spewing out of the window. We have a 200 mile journey ahead of us!" I think this is what you call a flash. "Was this your idea as well?" I said, "How can I justify taking credit for it, when I'm in Banff and you're in London?"

I sent George an sms and warned him my mate was gunning for him and to expect a hefty bill for cleaning the car. After he received that call he told me he was now a proud owner of a Golf GTI, but the only problem was it smelled of fish! I think after George got rid of it he was about 400£ out of pocket, quite an expensive prank, but one that sticks with you!

Passport

We were on our way to Amsterdam, six mates on a stag doo (a friend's last fling as a single bloke). We were quite excited waiting in Aberdeen airport even though it was 5am in the morning. At least we had the good old Scottish breakfast, square sausage, black pudding, eggs, bacon, and hash browns, great heart attack food, and washed it down with a pint of lager. As we were boarding the plane, George and myself were already scheming what we had in stall for my mate when we got there. Should we get him a stripper? I knew his future wife would go mental if she found out, but that was certainly a plan. During the flight, I went to the toilet and foolishly left my jacket on my seat, with my passport in it (schoolboy error) if there is an opening for a prank, please make sure your items are with you at all times, or prepare to suffer the consequences.

We arrived at passport control and as I approached, my mates were already through and George was there with a smile on his face. I thought, *why are these guys waiting around to for me?* I opened my passport at the picture page; I looked at it and burst out laughing. Someone (George) had drawn on my photo, permed hair, a moustache, and bushy eyebrows. It was something that resembled a Mexican drug baron, certainly nothing like the passport holder. I handed it across to the agent and as he double took, he said, that is not you, you cannot come into this country! I asked him to give it to me saying, "Do you really think I would have done this to my own passport?" I rubbed it out as it was a felt tip pen, not a ballpoint, even George wasn't that stupid. The agent said, "You must get new passport when you come back to your country!" I looked at George and told him I'd get him back.

Later during the trip, we were sat in a bar. George was busy speaking to these two girls. I saw an opportunity to get him back. I was sitting at the table when I saw the waitress going back to the bar with a teaspoon. On the tables there were candles. It wasn't really a romantic bar, so god only knows why there were candles there. I asked the waitress for the spoon and I held it underneath the candle, my mate asked what I was going to do with it. With a sly smile on my face, he knew I was up to no good. I walked over to George and stuck the hot spoon right in the middle of his forehead and instantly a blister appeared. Poor George! He ran over to the bar and got some ice from the bucket and placed it on his head and almost as fast as he did this a guy bumped into him and George replied, "Watch where you're going." The guy looked at him and said, "Ah, Cyclopes." A great comeback from a Dutch guy, not considered for their sense of humor. To this day, when he ventures into the sun, this area on his forehead goes a darker shade of pink. Scarred for life!

The funny thing was he was doing a training flight the following week and Captain Biggles, in a frightfully posh accent, said, "George, am going to have to ask you a question, what happened to your head?" George replied, "I fell asleep against the radiator."

Aviemore

Is a small village holiday resort in the Cairngorms, If anyone has been to this resort in the North of Scotland, you will understand what I'm talking about. I have been there on many occasions and they have all been eventful. I could actually write a book just on this place, but we will keep it to two stories. The first one was with George and the second story was with my nameless friend, Hey, we have all done things in the past that we choose not to mention. Life is life and without these experiences, who knows where it would have lead us?

It was during the summer of 1996, when I ventured up to the resort with two buddies, John and George. We arrived at our hotel and you could see the receptionist thinking, these three spell trouble!

Even at the check in we were giggling and scheming. You could see the girl was flustered as well as excited. She asked if we were tourists. "No, I am the owner's son," I piped up. I always had a quick answer, that's how my brain seems to work.

The girl looked at me and thought, this could be a good catch and maybe an early retirement for me. *Sorry*, I thought, *you're not my type*. After she handled all our details, she said, "If you like, there are a group of staff going out tonight after working hours, 11.30. We can meet you guys in the Highlander if you like?"

The three of us are never any guys to shy away from a party or an opportunity to meet some fresh girls, always a challenge to show your chat up skills. We went out for some food, George's shout, we all knew he would choose his favorite restaurant, Pizza land, quite a good franchise at the time. After that, we headed to the highlander and was amazed at the number of people in the bar. The ratio was around 1:1 so no worries there. When it came to talking to them, I went to the bar and a girl asked my name, just general chitchat. I don't understand people who fall for that shit. Girls who hang at the bars are looking for drinks and guys who buy them. Get real. I always have a way of throwing a curve ball, after the inevitable question, Scottish girls will ask if you want to buy them a drink. As soon as she said it, I replied think of a number between 1 and 7, generally people will always choose 7. She says 7, I then say wrong; you have to buy me a drink. If she comes over with a drink, then you have a good chance of getting these girls pants off. Try it, all you losers who buy women drinks. I have never bought a Woman a drink within 30 seconds of meeting her. You make the right choice of women then.

As we waited for the girls to arrive, the girls at the bar ventured over, drink in hand, gave it to me and walked away. I thanked her as she walked away. She must have been waiting for me to follow, but I declined. My two mates said she was well tidy and wanted to know why I didn't follow her. She will keep, I told them. That's my banker for the evening.

The girls from the hotel walked in. Another thing is, don't put all your cards on the table. There were some hot as chicks in this group, even the receptionist looked well. John asked the girls if they wanted a drink. George and me looked at each other and said, "Fail!"

The girls already seemed quite drunk and the receptionist said tonight was her leaving night. *Wow*, I thought, *easy targets*.

John seemed to be getting on well with the receptionist and we were not doing too badly with the others. As the night went on, we decided these would be a sure bet!

As we were leaving the girls said they couldn't come back to ours as they worked in the hotel and would lose their jobs if they went back with guests. We understood fully and the receptionist, it didn't matter anyway, she had left her job. We walked backed together, kissed the girls goodnight and thought always tomorrow, but at least we could have a laugh!

John was looking like a cat that has just got the cream. "Not often I have a girl and you two studs, end with nickets," he smiled. We had a rule whoever got the girl got the room. We were sharing the room and that was the rule! George and me were watching TV and I decided to get naked and go into the room, I switched on the light and John was looking relaxed, smoking a cig. The girl piped up and told me to get out. I picked up an orange that was on the dressing table and she said, "Give me that back, that is mine." From 12ft away and naked, I threw it in the air, headed it, chested it, and volleyed it and it hit her right on the forehead. I seriously couldn't do that again if I tried. What a shot. To this day, I think it's one of the funniest things I have ever done.

Hogmanay

This is the eve of New Year and a big occasion on any calendar, especially in Scotland. We would always head off or arrange a party depending on who was up for what.

One year, one of my friends had organized a trip to Aviemore. We set off with our girlfriends. We planned if we couldn't find accommodation; we had our tent with us. Bad move! We had arrived about 4pm and it was already snowing. We found a suitable spot and parked the car and went on the lookout for accommodation, the whole town was sold out. Other friends of ours were staying there, but the problem was their girlfriends simply didn't trust us. I wonder why.

It was 6pm when we pitched the tent. The snow was already quite thick and the thought of going out for a drink and retiring to this tent seemed a bit of a joke. We headed out for something to eat and went on a bar crawl. As the night grew older the girls stopped drinking as they were concerned about the weather. My mate and I continued drinking and when the bells rang in the New Year, we were all in this nightclub. It was around 1am and the girlfriends wanted to go back to the tent. We said ok and that we would be back in around an hour, as there was still some mischief to be had.

As we sat in this club after the girls had left, the plan was hatched. I went across to speak to a group of girls and as I chatted away, my mate just stood at the bar. The girls shouted at him to come over, women are like that always curious wondering why, people are not interacting. I replied he was just too shy and got nervous when there were girls around him. He eventually came across and as he sat down silent, the girls tried to coax him into the conversation. They kept saying, "He is cute. If he could speak to women, I am sure he would have his fair share."

After around 30 minutes, my mate kicked me under the table. This was the sign for me to go to the toilet. As I left, I said, "Please don't try and get him to talk as he is really nervous and something might happen." When I returned he was in full flow, the girls were all laughing at his jokes and humor. I said, "What have you done? I told you not to speak with him!" They were curious to why this was. I said look and pointed at his crotch. This was all a plan. He had deliberately pissed himself, the girls screamed and, of course, this was the cue for us to go back to the tent. When we arrived back the temperature had dropped to the minus and if we had fallen asleep in the tent, I am sure we would have been hypothermic. So we all huddled in the car, left the engine running and switched it off. When it got cold, we woke up and just repeated the cycle until early morning.

We drove home around 7 am, there were snow ploughs carving out single lanes on the road, but we managed to get home safely and live to tell another tale.

Driving around doing the circuit in Banff, always something eventful would happen.

Black Mac another one of Banff's characters. He was a wheeler-dealer and only seemed to have money during the summer months. Although he didn't stay in the famous Gallowhill, he was always over there, wheeling and dealing. I'm sure he was related to B&P or he definitely wouldn't have been allowed on that patch. Perhaps he bought the notables some drink.

The circuit in Banff and Macduff is a stretch of road in between the two towns, where if you have a car you drive aimlessly between both. On a particular evening during the summer, Pookie and me had just been to the gym. We saw Black Mac on his bike, cycling towards Banff. He was weaving across the road and it was quite obvious he was under the influence. As we passed him, he almost clipped the car with shock that someone was passing him. I didn't think he was wearing a yellow jersey and competing in the 'tour de Banff ', but I might have been mistaken. I said to Pookie, "Let's do one more circuit and this time, when we go behind Black Mac, we slow down and blast the horn!" As we passed him going the other direction, I noticed he had a cigarette in his mouth and peddling away, probably singing to himself. Pookie did a three-point turn and headed towards him, slowed down, and switched off his engine so Black Mac wouldn't hear anything. I think he had a Walkman on, listening to Queen, I want to ride my bicycle, but I might be mistaken. Pookie blasted the horn and Black Mac swerved and hit the pavement, falling off his bike, and cigarette still in his mouth. If you could see his face, it was like a Rembrandt. I thought Pookie was going to crash his car and my stomach was in knots from laughing so hard. I don't think I have ever laughed so much. Well that's a lie, when Rangers went into administration, I defiantly laughed harder.

Pookie parked the car at Banff Bridge, because that's how far we could travel for laughing, we saw him cycling past, looking stunned. We decided to follow him and see if we could do something else! He stopped at the market for a half decker and a chaser, probably too embarrassed to tell the folk in the bar why his knuckles were scrapped. He was sitting there innocently wondering how and why this had happened, then Pookie and me decided to hatch another plan. We knew his last pub visit would be the Central, (formally known as Ma Black's), the pub of which a good friend of ours owned. We went to the bar for a game of pool and a soft drink and spoke to the owner's son, young Billy. We asked him if he had a shifting spanner, a very strange thing to be asking someone at 10.30pm on a Tuesday evening unless you wanted to get up to mischief, I suppose, which we were, of course. We told Billy our plan and off he ventured to his Dad's toolbox. His father was Iconic in the community, a hardworking and respected man. He tragically died in a roofing accident some years later, a very sad day for both towns. Billy returned with the tool and we waited for Black Mac to arrive in the bar. He would always park his bike out front of the bar on the pavement, leaning against the wall. I tell you this; I have no idea how someone can cycle after doing a pub crawl. It amazes me! After a pub-crawl, I could barely walk; maybe that's why it's called crawl! We waited until Black Mac had about two mouthfuls left in his drinks and then we went outside and loosened the front wheel enough so that it would fall off as he descended to the road. In theory, we hoped it would pan out that way!

Sure as death, out he came, mounted his bike, and as he disembarked the pavement. The front wheel fell off, forks in the road and fell over. Bloody hilarious. Young Billy was rolling about laughing his head off, another story for him to tell his friends.

Pic 1: Duff House The Famous Haunted House in Banff, where the 'Green lady resides'

Pic 2: Duff House Royal Golf Club

Pic 3: Banff Bridge where we took a skinny dip walking home one early morning.

Pic 4: Support your Local Team Deveronvale.

Chapter 7

The Local Pubs

We had a great local pub called the 'Aul Fife' and a pretty handy Sunday football team. It was perfect for me. Rugby on the Saturday, football on a Sunday - an ideal scenario. The team we had was good, 'toy boy' (Robbie Keith) up front, he was a finisher, had a great eye for goal, and one on one he was deadly. I was on the right wing, supplier and finisher - a good combination. We had the Hen (Nomie), in mid-field. What an engine this boy had; up and down, he was certainly our Beckham. Connell, on the left, he was the type of player that never knew what he was going to do himself and would grab a goal as well. We had two great guys in midfield/defense. Tarzie was about 5ft 6inch, but could out jump many 6ft players. What a spring he had in his step. He certainly could have played at a higher level, but some way along the track he got involved in the drug scene and ended up hanging himself. Tragic, really. We also had another great left sided player, Andy Main (Mabel) he did play at a higher level, albeit for a short time, but work commitments never really allowed him to further his footballing career. He unfortunately died in an offshore accident.

It was about this time I started to think there was life outside Banff, the small Northeast town where I grew up and had so many memories. I went to the local job center/dole office where I used to wait in the queue fortnightly and saw so many of Banff's characters. Although I saw myself as a character, I didn't want to be one of these, especially a guy called, 'Cakie Burnett'; he was the likable rogue. I always remember the time previously incident involving the cleaning fluid.

I spoke to the job center women and asked if there were any job positions outside of the town. She was curious, as she knew I played rugby and loved it, and she asked, "What about Rugby?" I replied, "The season is over, if I don't like the job, then I can always come back home." I applied for a job as a kitchen porter in 'British Home Stores' and stayed with my brother, about 20 minutes to my work by bus every day! It was during the summer months and my other brother asked me to play for his local village side. They were playing in the summer leagues in Aberdeen so I said, "Why not, it will keep me fit for the Rugby season." I started to feel better about playing football again and switched to playing more. I had a season out of Rugby and started playing semi-pro football, but it wasn't the same. I missed the general discipline of Rugby and the comradely, something that's not around in football.

I worked in Aberdeen for nearly two years, but was feeling a little homesick even though I went home every Friday night.

The Aul Fife was a great pub, the landlord, John, was a likeable bachelor and certainly knew how to run a business, he fancied himself as a ladies man, so at least we had one thing in common. We had so many memories of that bar and if I could think of the business we brought to that place, it would be scary. We would practically live there on the weekends, which started on Friday evening. Down we would go to the bar and play pool, cards, or darts. I still, to this day, don't get why women come to the bars. Oh wait, to get drunk and maybe because we were there.

In the bar there was quite a unique feature - a huge fish tank. On Saturday's, people would go across to the local pet store and buy a few fish for the tank. I am sure the owners of both facilities would have a say in this, one Saturday afternoon we were playing pool and I was up next. Although the stakes weren't high if you lost, the bragging rights were that you gained street cred! I remember starting the game well and giving away a foul shot, where Robbie proceeded to clear the table. I didn't like getting beat at the best of times, but losing to Robbie wasn't the best. He was not the best pool player, but he was one of the luckiest. I rifled the white ball off the cushion in anger as the game was over, it then struck the cue, which had been left on the table and flew right towards the Fish Tank. It was like slow motion, the ball hit the bottom corner, a six-inch hole appeared and the water started pouring onto the floor, luckily enough no one was sitting at the table. If it had been later that evening when the place was packed, a different scenario would have occurred. John the barman/owner shot out from the bar with one of these huge empty flip bins. He acted quickly as the bin started to fill, it was then he did something extraordinary and, to this day, he must be confused by his actions. He opened the door and emptied the contents of the bucket in the gutter. All the fish headed down the sewer. Maybe there are some mutant sewer fish still living there to this day. When John entered the bar again, he was puzzled why he had carried out such an action. The only thing that survived the fish tank escapade were the turtles, and for my involvement I was banned from the bar for two weeks, but I was allowed in on Sundays to run and organize the pub football team. Who else would go around getting the semi-hung-over players from their beds?

We had quite a handy football side; 40% of the team played for 'Banff Rovers' and anyone who knew who the Rovers were understood how good we were. I'm not just saying that. Even the local higher-level sides struggled against the Rovers.

The Rovers drank out of the Tolbooth, a bar at the foot of the strait path. I don't know why the street was called the straight path, as the hill was so firkin steep!

Roy and Sandra were the owners of those premises. Roy was an ex-army guy and didn't particular like the hilarity. He also had another job working offshore, two weeks on, two weeks off. When he was at home he seemed to be always working and looked as if he deserved a break, but the guy was a workaholic.

Sandra was a little more forgiving and she liked the humor that we brought to the bar and, of course, the business. It was a family run affair. Her sister and mother were the cooks, their great Scottish home cooking and their bar lunches were to die for. They did excellent cheese salads with huge portions, but my favorite was lasagna.

On Saturday and Sundays they sometimes had live bands and there was a great mix of clientele; rockers, mods, bikers. One time during a mate's visit, the drinks were flowing. There was this hot chick (can't remember her name) but I remember the dog's name, Sookie. She loved that dog; she took it everywhere. I remember Gas, an English bloke who was in our company, he was petting the dog, so the girl was cool about the situation. He started to rub the dog's balls. It was getting excited, as any man would do if this was happening, then he started stroking the dog's penis. We started to laugh and, of course, the owner didn't find it funny. All hell broke loose. The girl stood up and slapped the guy across the face (as any true dog lover would do). Gas, coolly said, "F**k off, bitch. Just because the dog is getting an orgasm and you've never had one." Sandra asked us to leave quietly. God knows what would have happened if Roy had been there.

The Central bar (formally Ma Blacks) was an iconic bar at bottom of the gallowhill; a gold mine in its day, as this was the only bar that would allow people credit, where soon as you had your Giro (social security check) and you cleared part of your tab, you could get another drink. When I was still in the primary school, I remember walking past there and so many characters were in that bar, non-other than Ma Black herself, not related to Black Hughie. I heard stories that this bar was the only bar that would allow you in, even if you had been banned from all the others. It was the last stop shop, the final bar for a dram, before you went up the street to face the music from the wife or girlfriend.

Another Great character was Baxi, he was like a father to me and was very friendly with his sons. He was a legend in himself, a local who you didn't mess with. He was very friendly with my Dad, but totally different in so many ways. He put his family before Alcohol, unlike my Dad, (After 30 years of putting his body through a half-decker and a chaser, he finally gave up drink). I am sure he is a better man for it now, but I don't think I have seen my dad for at least 15 years.

I was happy when Baxi and his wife, Sylvie, bought the central. The whole town knew this would be a special bar, especially because of his character. His wife Sylvie was a gem and you were always welcome in her house, especially for her tattie soup. My friend, Stuart, was home on leave and he was helping his dad build the bar. They had a huge dog, called Boson. He was a Rottweiler and certainly a great guard dog, the sort of dog that would invite you into the house to burgle it and then turn into the exorcist, (*you can't leave I want to play*). Many a time, when Stu and Baxi were on the roof, the dog would let you in and then stand in front of the door. As you would try and gently coax it away from the door with your leg, he would look at you and tease you, that goddam dog weighed 80kg. I remember one time it was walking across the wall that ran alongside the bar. The wall was about 15ft; Boson fell off and landed on his side. I'm sure he broke the pavement. Only kidding, he just stood up, shook himself, and walked away.

On one occasion, I had just returned from holiday in Greece. I popped into see a friend where he worked and we went out with a group of his friends in their local town. One of his friends was having a leaving run. He was leaving his job and the guys had decided it was a bloke's only night. If we were caught chatting to women, then we would have to suffer the consequences. As the night grew on, I went to the toilet and saw these two girls sitting by themselves. I decided to try and speak to them. It was only going to be 10 minutes; the guys wouldn't even know I was gone. One of my mates friend sneaked up behind us and climbed onto the back of the bar sofa. We still didn't notice, as it was quite dark. I felt something warm run down my shoulder and I looked up and jumped at the same time. The guy was pissing down my back and it was bouncing off the women. He just said, "You know the rules, no speaking to women." I retired back to the group.

The next day we travelled back to Banff in a friend's car. We arrived home around 6pm. The plan was to get a quick shower and head out for something to eat and that was it for the night. We had to make the most of the evening, as he would be driving back to the base on Sunday and I was desperate to show my tan off. It normally only lasted a week in Scotland, simply because of the weather.

The evening went as any other normal Friday. The town was always quiet because not much ever happened on a Friday. The big day was always Saturday evening.

I went home around 12 o'clock and my mother had been waiting up for me. As I walked in the door, you could see she was ready to burst. I recall her using such language only when she was severely pissed off. She said, "What the hell is that in your trouser pocket?" I looked stunned and totally oblivious to what she was talking about. She told me that someone put shit in my pocket. She wasn't sure who did it, perhaps one of my friend's mates, as I knew he wouldn't do something like that, but he was going to pay for it.

I apologized and went out of the house. I walked down to his parents stayed. Just along the street was a local park, where people walked their dogs. I found this bucket and spade (for building sandcastles). Of course, I was going to build 'shitcastles' I collected a whole pale of shit and went and smeared it on every panel of my mate's car. Revenge was smelly.

The next day we had planned a bike run. I cycled down to his house and was met by his father. I asked where my mate was. His Dad looked pissed off to say the least. He replied, "Do you know anyone that has a grudge against my son?" I looked puzzled and confused; I was really good at covering my guilt and could keep a straight face. I just replied, "No, why?" He said, "Someone has covered his car with shit and, I tell you this, if I find out who it was, I personally will kill him." I asked again where Stu was. His dad told me he was at the garage power washing his car.

As I approached him, he just smiled and said, "You know I wouldn't do something like that to you", I questioned why did his friends have to do it then?

Another local was the St. Andrew's. This was a nightclub where I had done some DJ Work. I would never consider myself a DJ, but I knew music and I knew the floor fillers.

I was more of a nightclub person because I liked a place where I could socialize and talk to girls. I had the best chat up line on record, "Do you want to come back to my place for a swim?"

Working as a Supervisor at the local swimming pool had its benefits and skinny-dipping was certainly one of them. I would always talk to women who were unlikely to vomit in the pool. I didn't fancy taking the pool hoover out at 3am and cleaning anything, so usually I knew by talking to them if they would fit the bill.

If I was lucky, I would jump in a taxi with the girl and we would stop just before the pool at the house opposite and wait until the coast was clear then enter by the back door, quickly disarm the building, pull the pool cover back around 5 meters, then strip off and go for a swim with my date. Those were fun times and god only knows why I was never caught.

One of the owner's of the St. Andrew's owned a bar in the next town, called the Bayview. This was a bar everyone frequented after hours, usually for a nightcap (afterhours drink). This was totally illegal and probably why there were only a select few allowed in the bar afterhours, blokes and girls not likely to fight or cause a nuisance. In the front bar there was a pool table, which was also where the women's toilets were. Everyone used to congregate in the lounge. This area had tinted windows so the local police couldn't see in. I was there with Billy, as he was attracted to a local girl. When she showed no interest (as his chat up lines were lacking) we decided to go and play pool. *Boring*! No, we played the game naked. The first chick came through to the toilet and was quite shocked. She then told the other girls, Ron and Billy are through there playing naked pool!

Then the owner came through and suggested we put our clothes back on. I replied, "After we finish the game." It was time to leave and was around 4.30am. I said to Billy, "Let's walk home naked. Not wanting to be black catted, we both walked home. When you live in a small town, you can get away with shit like this, especially because there was no traffic on the roads at those time (Sunday Morning). As we approached Banff Bridge, I said, "Look, the tide is low. Why don't we walk across the river naked?" I can only imagine if someone saw us carry that out. We would have been driven in strait jackets to Cornhill (the mental hospital).

The last bar was probably the busiest in the two towns. The Castle had a good mix of people; young and old would frequent the bar. During my Rugby playing days, I worked in the bar on Friday evening and when I worked weekends at the pool, I worked Saturday night, as the pool wasn't a great place to be on a Sunday morning with a Hangover!

There was an evening in the summer where the bar was not busy. This was typical, when there was the Foggie Flower show or the Turriff show. Everybody would be at these events. The bar staff started playing around with the security pen (this signified if the bank note was legal) the writing would only show up under a florescent light. We were surprised when two girls came into the bar. They were not from the area, they also looked quite shocked at the empty bar.

While chatting to the girls they were curious as to why we were writing on each with a security marker. I suggested we could write something on you if you like. She agreed.

I winked at her friend and said to the unsuspecting girl, "I will write 'smile if you think am sexy'." She said, "Oh, that's sweet." What I wrote was 'smile if you want a fuck'. Her friend gave me the thumbs up, they had a quick drink, and left. I ventured along to the nightclub and saw the girls on the dance floor, loads of blokes were circling them, acting like male lion's. They were all smiling at the girl for obvious reasons. Well, you do have to amuse yourselves when the bar is quiet.

Back Row: John; Nommie; Gary; Sean (on beer crate) Stu; Neil; Dave

Front Row: Neil; Davie; Me; Robbie C; Gary; Robbie K

Chapter 8

Wingmen and Holidays

Having mates in all walks of life, opened doors for fun and practical jokes. I will not mention any of my friend's names's as some are respected member of society, but many people reading this book will know exactly whom I'm referring too!

Growing up together, he decided after serving his apprenticeship, he decided to follow his grandfather's footsteps.

He went away for training and you could see he was apprehensive. I gave him some sound advice and said this was a great opportunity for him to travel and see the world. He breezed through the training and passed with flying colors. His family was excited to go to his passing out ceremony and he certainly came back a different person, but for the better. Of course, it set him in the right direction.

He obviously spoke highly of his hometown and of the characters we had there and his army mates certainly felt this when they visited.

There are many stories, some funny and some weird and distasteful.

One time during a home leave visit, we arranged to meet at our local bar, the Tollbooth. I remember meeting with his father (god rest his soul). We were walking along the street and saw a group of women; they were with some biker lads. As we approached, everything kicked off, a full-scale fight had broken out. The women started fighting with the bikers; handbags, shoes, and lipstick were flying everywhere. I stopped his father and said, "Let's just wait a minute." He looked puzzled. I continued, "That's your son and his mates fighting with that biker gang." He shook his head. We let the dust settle and within the space of five minutes we were all in the bar, bikers included, having a drink and a laugh. It was times like that, mobile camera phones would have been handy.

On another occasion, I went down to see him for a weekend. He said they had a trip to Edinburgh planned and was going to be fancy dress. I was used to dressing up, it was a regular occurrence during rugby trips; fancy dress, bus runs, etc.

We arrived in Edinburgh early 9.30 am, found a bar in Leith, and arranged to meet back there at 12pm. Then we all went shopping and, of course, the theme was women. There were 22 of us. I was the only civvy (civilian) most blokes thought I was in the military and said I had the same mindset.

We met back at the bar and changed into dresses, miniskirts, lipstick, shoes, handbags, necklaces, and earrings; tough being a chick. We had arranged to do a bungee jump off a 140ft crane, dressed as women. Laughs were defiantly in order.

The owner of the bar welcomed the business and said, "Guys, if you would like a drink after the bungee jump, you are more than welcome back here, as there won't be many bars that will let you in, especially on a Friday at 5pm." We did the jump, all survived and were stoked, and then we made our way across the street and started to queue outside the bar. It was jammed packed, but the doormen gave us VIP treatment. We entered the bar like rock stars, but something wasn't quite right. As I scanned the bar, I noticed some weird and wonderful characters in the premises. It was then I realized it was a gay bar a great piece of marketing from the owner, come back here, phone his mates, and the cash register is full.

There were many propositions in that bar, but I can assure you everyone left unscathed.

The next time we dressed up was to be in our hometown. We went to Aberdeen to a place called Party Mania. We hired two costumes, a horse that required two people and a bin man, which required one. So three of us ventured across to the next town, where havoc would prevail. If you picture the scene, there's a packed bar and in walks a horse followed by a bin man. Of course they could recognize the bin man, but not the horse. They just put two and two together and realized it was the three amigos.

We decided the bar was too crowded and waited outside the next bar instead. We decided to chase everyone who came out of the bar. Well, women, of course. The men might have got physical, the women just screamed. These times are great memories and cannot be taken away from me. Living life to its fullest is the best medicine.

Everyone remembers the three degrees. Well, not everyone. One day the three amigos went into Aberdeen and bought some theatrical paint, along with some flares, flowery shirts, and medallions, and, of course, the 70's footwear - platform shoes, made famous by the Bay City Rollers. *Bye Bye Baby* was their hit song. A Scottish tartan clad band, they were almost as popular as the Beatles.

The theatrical paint was brown colored paint, as we were dressing up as black guys. Some might say that would be a racist statement; I say wise up, some people talk life too seriously.

We had three Afro wigs and black sunglasses to hide our identity, but little did we know, this would be the most eventful night the small town of Banff had ever witnessed. We decided to have a few beers before we went out. As we ventured across the street to the local Spar, I was waiting outside and a father and mother stopped outside the shop; the son was inside. I could see the father staring at me and the other guy, totally oblivious to who we were. I approached the car and, with my best Jami can accent, I said, "Hello there, man." The father, being his usual witty self, said, "Not bad yourself."

Then a distraught mother came out and said, "This most ignorant black person came up to me in the shop and said, "Hello there, mama." Not knowing this was her son, as I removed my glasses and wig to reveal our identity, they both had a side-splitting moment.

The son came out and said, "Hello mam" fit like.

We knew then this would be a great night. If the mother and father couldn't recognize us, who would?

We went into the Tollbooth around 7.30, which was earlier than normal, told the bar staff who we were, and sat opposite. You could see the regulars asking whom the hell these were guys. We had for warned the staff to say we were off a cargo boat, who had just delivered some coal and we were the workers on that vessel. Looking different and acting different was easy on our part. For the regular customers, it was change. Most people don't like change and as there was only one black family in the town, seeing three black people was a big deal.

We found most of the people that came to see us were girls. I think they thought we could offer them something different, something thicker and longer. Luckily, we couldn't oblige, as neither of us could come across with such lengths and girths.

The next stop was the market where we actually met one of Banff's characters. Black Hughie was a white bloke who worked at the coal sheds filling the coal sacks for the lorries to deliver to heat the houses of the local community. The reason why he was called Black Hughie is he didn't like to wash, because his bath was full of coal. I had a lot of admiration for him; he was a hardworking man, but his kids were social scroungers, all three of them never had a job in their lives. He worked himself to an early grave just to support his family.

The three degrees were on fire, pulling out some great dance moves and everyone wanted to know our identity. We had a following, all the chicks were following us from bar to bar and where the chicks went, so did the guys. We were in this particular bar and the co-owner was also the owner of the second nightclub in the town, which was closed for renovation. He approached us and said, "Look guys, I know who you are. Would it be possible for you to make a guest appearance next month to open the nightclub?" We said yes, of course, but wanted to know what rewards we'd get. For them to get the real three degrees would cost a fortune, but we said we'd do it for slightly cheaper.

We used to look forward to the Turriff show every year, it was a great opportunity to play jokes, even if it did land you in serious trouble. The first stop was always the showground. The beer tent was always full to the max, and this year was no different. Usually we would go there around 2pm and see all the drunken farmers trying to find themselves a wife. I wonder how many relationships started and ended in that beer tent.

We wouldn't start drinking at that time, but we would go in and see old friends (ex-rugby colleagues) and they would try and humiliate me by challenging me to an arm wrestle. I will never get that mentality, people showing off or trying to impress friends and potential wives, by challenging the same sex to an arm-wrestle. When did this become a bedroom show of strength? Let's have an arm wrestle, before we have sex!

When these shows of strength started, I knew it was time for me to go for a walk. Walking around the showground gave you a chance to eye the talent that would be on show that evening. I was talking about the Mairs Suffolks (famous sheep breeders in Turriff) and the sheep with the golden balls. These sheep would sell for the equivalent of a small semi-detached house in the area. As the day grew on, we went back to the beer tent and this time the young farmers were slowly decreasing and the more interesting pieces of eye candy came in, dressed in their best frocks and wellie boots, because it always rained at the show. The drinks started to flow and so did the banter. We always approached these girls, especially the ones that didn't want an arm wrestle. We were in full conversation and the barmen and women shouted for last orders. We had our final drink and headed up to the local nightclub. There was a group of girls following us and they asked us to slow down so we could have a chat and a smooch. One of the girls asked if I could wait because she wanted to go into the portaloo (these were portable toilets used at these type of events; easy to clean and transport friendly). As the girl stepped into the toilet, we all waited patiently and hung around. This is the time when am at my most dangerous, given time to think of what kind of hilarity I could bring. I approached the portaloo where the girl was sitting and proceeded to push it over. This was a great show of strength, more impressive than any arm wrestle in my books. I made that up. I think a five-year-old boy could have done it. Her friends were in totally shock, especially as she removed herself from the upturned tardis. She was fuming to say the least and off course covered from head to foot in the contents of the portaloo, I guess she wasn't smooching anyone that night. Then again, maybe she met a farmer on the way home.

I didn't have too many fans when playing practical jokes. I just liked being different.

When I look back on some of the things we have done in bars and clubs, I wouldn't be proud of my kid doing such things, but I guess everyone has their moments; some regrets, some laughs, and some what the hell.

We had been on a stag night in another town, when I asked the Guys if they wanted to play a game called 'Ride the Elephant'. Some were reluctant, but others agreed. I explained the rules.

You find the biggest girl on the dance floor and you ask her for a dance.

You are required to dance with her for at least two dances.

You then approach her from behind and slip your arms under her armpits.

You then jump on her back and say you can't believe how big she is, in a not so nice manner.

That's when the clock starts, you hold on for as long as it takes her to throw you off her back.

One of the guys was holding on for grim life and the girl reared up like buckaroo, which was a kid's game we all had or played at least once in our lives. He was catapulted across and landed on a table full of drinks. The game was over and so was our night.

It was 1989 when I first decided to venture overseas for a two-week holiday. I chose a Greek holiday island called Corfu.

I remember my brother driving me down to Glasgow Airport for me to catch my first ever plane flight. It was a little rehab, recoup. People thought it was weird me going on holiday alone! It's sometimes best being on your own, it gives you time to think!

When I arrived on this idyllic island, I was amazed how laid back everyone was. I now realize why the Greek economy has failed. Breakfast time was buzzing, but lunch was a little more subdued as most of the tourists were away on trips or sleeping off their binge drinking. Lunch was like something from the ok coral prior to a gunfight – slow, easy and waiting for something to happen. So after lunch the locals went for the customary siesta, just about the time some budget travelers were heading to the beach to top off a tan or chat up some nice women.

During the flight, I met a couple of guys from the South of Scotland. They had a good sense of humor and I thought why not hangout with them, as we enjoyed each other's company. We went on this boat trip, beach barbeque, eyeing up the talent. I spotted this stunner in her bikini, with a bronzed body to die for or die on. As we arrived at our destination, I said a brief hello to her. The guys thought I was crazy to approach such a beautiful woman. I noticed she was with a girl that wasn't the best looking girl (a munter). This was a typical scenario on holiday, couples or groups with either stunners or munters, trying to get laid on holiday.

The tour reps were busy setting up food for everyone and most people were swimming, reading, or getting on it (drinking). This was a regular occurrence for the package type holidays, binge drinking. We were on it and when I am on it, there will always be a prank on the make. I saw the opportunity with this girl, as she lay her round, not rectangular, towel down on the sand. She strode across the beach showing her body, like a dog in heat! As she entered the water and swam out, with the munter following, trying to get more beautiful as she swam, the plan was hatched. I quickly move to the towel and dug a hole, the depth of around a meter. I was moving the sand like a beaver on speed. I placed the towel neatly over the hole and waited! As she was strutting across the beach, everyone watching, she sat down on the towel and folded like a badly set up deck chair. The group was laughing like crazy; you could also see the glint in the munters eye! As she helped to pull her out of the hole. She kept a low profile during the rest of the trip, then, on the way back on the bus she had her Walkman on and switched of to what was going on around her.

It was around 6pm when we arrived back and we agreed to meet at 10pm and we would be on it again. Sometimes you would just sleep right through until 12 and not bother going out. As I was only there for 10 days, I wanted to make the most of it! I met the guys at Spiro's kebab shop, a good place to eat and see what the flow of talent was like. I saw the stunner and her friend. She was looking more and more stunning. I don't care what people say, a pasty white female is not attractive! Show me a tanned beauty and hands down they win. As she went into the bar, I suggested to the guys as we left Spiro's, "Let's go in here for a change." The guys said there is Tracy. I went, "Who the hell is that?" The girl on the trip, Simon replied. I could see she had a few drinks and there were some guys talking to her friend. This is a usual occurrence. When guys are trying to talk to her friend to get the nice girl's attention. I said to Simon, "I am going to talk to her and tell her it was me that did the towel scenario to her this morning!" She was leaning against the bar with a drink in her hand and I said, "Would you like to buy me a drink?" She replied, "Who are you and why should, I buy you a drink?" "Well I'm the guy that dug the hole that your butt fitted into this morning." "Oh my god, I can't believe you did that to me, it was so funny to look back on!"

She bought me a drink, and then I thanked her for it and walked back to my mates! The guys wanted to know how the hell she bought me a drink. I said, "You make a girl smile or make a joke, she will be back. You see the guy around her now, he has probably been trying her all holiday." Simon replied, "He is the water-ski instructor. An English guy who thinks he's cool."

I approached, again and she said, "You're back, glad to see you." She also whispered in my ear, "This guy is a jerk, but would you like to go waterskiing tomorrow?" I hesitated, and then told her I had only tried it once but I would give it another go. She asked the guy and he said, it wasn't a problem. As he left, he gave me the thumbs up, as if to say I'd be alright. I asked Tracey, where she was going to next. She was going home, as it had been a long and stressful day. I asked about her friend. Tracey said her friend would bring that guy back to the apartment once she was drunk and give him a good time! I said is that what you're going to do with me? She looked at me and said, "Walk me home and you'll find out!"

The next day, we met at Spiro's. The guys still didn't believe me about last night, but as she walked through the door and came across and kissed me on the cheek, they quickly changed their opinions. We walked across to the beach and the guy was there, warming up the boat. I had watched him a few times during the holiday, showing of his bronzed body, but I had one on him, but I somehow thought he would get his own back. As we arrived at the waterskiing spot, I kind of thought it wasn't going to be fun. I put my skis on and stepped into the water and the guy asked if I had skied before. I said, not really! He smiled and told me I'd be all right. I held on to the guide rope and was just about to get out of the water when he gunned it and I was flat on my face. He came round again I picked the rope and, as I was out of the water, he slowed down. This continued for a few more attempts. I was getting more and more pissed off, so I decided to call it quits. As I climbed back into the boat, Tracey looked pissed off as well, the guy was laughing, saying, "I thought you could ski mate!"
Upon reaching the beach, Tracey said, "I'll see you at Spiro's" I looked at the guy and said, "Mate, I have done in

one day what you couldn't do in one and half weeks." He wanted to know what I meant. "I shagged her last night and she was good." The little chance he had with her was out of the window; just because of the way he made a fool of me. I arrived in Spiro's, she said, "What an asshole. What was he thinking, he could have drowned you?" I replied, "Well, it's obvious he wants to sleep with you." "He has very little chance of that," she said. "I'm leaving tomorrow. But you can be with me tonight again, if you want."

I fell in love with Greece. To me it was the most idyllic place in the world, until I visited Indonesia, of course.

Greece was surreal; beautiful sunsets and beautiful holidaymakers that wanted to be loved and taken advantage of. It was 1990; I was in my prime and had the body of a Greek Adonis. Well so I thought. After my leg break, I decided I needed to show off my pecs. I had been going to the gym for almost 16 months. This was off-season for the rugby and I was in recovery mode and waiting for the season to start again. I liked my own company, I always have. Sometimes it's better to be alone and not have too many ideas floating around. I asked my brother to take me to the airport. As I was standing in the queue, I spotted a couple of guys and the banter was flowing between them. I waited till I checked in and asked them where they were going and what place they were staying at. They replied, "We are going to Kavos." (Greece's answer to Ibiza). I said, "Me too, do you mind if I tag along with you guys? It was so easy to make friends on holiday; people seem to lose all their inhibitions. When you go on holiday there always seems to be a stunning girl, with a not so stunning friend or two, or two stunners and a friend that some blokes feel sorry for and take advantage of. I would talk to anyone, but I had certain standards when it came to pulling girls. Usually I would approach the stunner and depending on who was my wingman, he would talk to the friend. We were on a beach barbeque party and everyone was bikinied up and the guys wore their best speedos (budgie smugglers). I had a pair of white cycling shorts. I liked to be different. Wear different clothes and you get noticed more. Or people shout faggot. Either way, that type of thing doesn't bother me. Sticks and stones and all that jazz.

During another Greek holiday to the Island of Crete, with two friends, this was one of the funniest holidays I have ever been on. We only went for one week, but every day there was a funny incident. It all started in the trip from the airport. Our holiday rep was Simon. To qualify for a Holiday rep, you need to be nuts, constantly wired (as if you were on narcotics 24/7), and be able to sell snow to Eskimos. Simon met all these three. He approached the three guys sitting at the back of the bus gingerly. You could see by the look in his eye, we could spell trouble, events, and experiences he could tell his friends, but certainly not his grandchildren.

As he spoke to us in his thick Geordie accent, he was curious to know why only two of us were involved in the conversation. This of course was a pre-planned scenario from us. He pointed at the quiet guy and asked why he wasn't talking. I said he was deaf and dumb (of course he wasn't). Simon was so apologetic and profusely apologized. He was embarrassed to say the least. I said, "Don't worry, he won't hear you." He sort of laughed. Simon then asked if we were interested in going on any trips, such as Greek night, Pub Crawl, and boat party. I said hell yeah and the deaf guy will pay for all three. He looked shocked again and then quickly realized he couldn't hear.

I said his parents have gave us 500GBP to spend on trips and we were going to spend and drink all our mate's money, cause he was a wanker and we didn't like him anyway. If you saw Simons face. He was amazed we could talk about a friend in that way. As the insults were growing, Simon gave my mate the thumbs up and went away down the front of the bus, sort of shaking his head in disbelief. I shouted, "Simon, where do we sign up for these trips?" He said, "Tomorrow we will come to your hotel at 10am."

When we arrived at the hotel and left the bus, my deaf and dumb mate passed Simon and gave him the thumbs and then produced a cigarette and said, "You got a lite, mate?" Simons face was a picture, the kind when you have been black catted, a mixture of emotion and amazement. He shook his head and knew we would be trouble.

We met the next day and booked the three trips, the first one was the pub crawl, with a talent show in the last bar, 200 people with the same thought on their mind, to have fun and take things to another level.

As usual, these things started off quiet, everyone sizing up the situation and talent, of course. One of my mates said, "We have a part to play in this talent show." I thought neither of us could sing, dance, or were confidant to do stand up. My mate said, "We are going to call ourselves the 'Waterboys'." I was puzzled at first and said, "Aren't they a Scottish band?"

The plan started. We entered the talent show and Simon wasn't sure what our theme was or how to announce our entry onto the stage. We had three rules prior to our entry, we were allowed no toilet visits, we played a game of spoof just before, and nobody was allowed to back out.

As we retreated to prepare ourselves for the dramatic entry, one mate said we all have to be naked on stage. We played the game of spoof and I won! When we came onto stage all naked we could hear the audience going crazy. Now I know how a rock star feels and this was only 200. Can you imagine thousands? We took our positions: mate 1 sitting, mate 2 kneeling, and myself standing. We were stacked like champagne glasses. I was to start the fountain. It was like the fountains of Bellagio in Vegas. As I started to piss on my mates, the audience was laughing. Then mate 2 started, people were taking pictures left right and center. They couldn't get close enough. I then started to pee in my hand and throw it over the audience. The crazy things you do when you are young.

We went around the back to get changed and Simon came in and said, "Fucking amazing. Five years as a tour rep and that's the best talent show yet." The next bar, Simon went straight to the DJ Booth and announced us and proceeded to tell our story. He said, "If there any Welsh, Irish, or English guys who can better that, then come up here and show us what you've got." Not to be black catted, we said we have another party piece, so we played spoof again. This time, I lost the bet, so the forfeit was on me. I asked what we were playing for. He smiled and said I had to drink a pint of his piss. I thought, *fuck sake*, but agreed. That's how we rolled as mates. We said to Simon, "Announce this across the DJ Booth." When he did, people were in disbelief. Why the hell would anybody do such a thing, must be mad. The crowd started to gather, and then my mate produced this warm, slightly colored, full glass of piss. There were two girls sitting next to me, they said, "That can't be what the guy says it is, why the hell are you going to drink that?" I said, "I lost the bet." To this day, I don't know why I managed to empty the contents down my throat and into my stomach, but what I do remember is the two girls' faces and the projectile vomit that came from their mouths. I just took a swig of beer and tried not to think too much about it, I never vomited, god knows why not!

Later on that evening I spoke with a girl, who wasn't sure of what we had done. We chatted normal and ended up kissing. My breath must have been really bad and I wonder what the hell she was thinking. She went back to her apartment, as we both had had too much to drink, but we agreed to meet at the beach the following afternoon. The next day on the beach we met along with the other lads, then we spotted Simon. He was bouncing with excitement as if he had just won the lottery. He said, "Guys, that was unbelievable last night. It was the best and I spoke with the head tour rep and she would like to meet you." I thought, *oh shit, this is Simon getting us back for the first meeting in the bus.* He said the company would like you to perform that act on stage at our end of year convention at Skegness, in front of 5000 people. What do you think? I was definitely up for it. The girl who I had kissed the previous evening looked shocked and said, "You guys did what?" Then when Simon told her about the piss incident, she picked her things up and left. I couldn't blame her really, but hey ho, that's how we roll.

The next trip was the Greek night, where you went into the suburbs in the Hills and had food at a famous venue; a local Greek family always ran this. It was all-commercial, of course. We were about to leave the bus and Simon, pipes up and says, "As a matter of respect, would everyone remove his or her shoes?" We were first off the bus, and made our way across to get our picture taken with the Greek dancers. I noticed everyone had his or her shoes on. Simon smiled; I guess he thought this was a black cat. He was way below our standards. Three guys from the North East of Scotland weren't about to be outdone by a Geordie, give him his due he tried. As I stood next to the dancers, I said to my mates, "I have my dick out and it will be in the picture" They said, "No f**king way." We then went and had a shot of ouzo, a drink that tastes of aniseed balls, a boiled sweet I used to eat as a kid, but of course having too much of this would get you extremely drunk, along with the grappa (sediment of wine). We started to dance the Zorba and we all linked arms. When we were in full flow, I took my dick out, and when Simon spotted it, he shot up and pulled me to the side and said they would kill me if they saw that shit. I couldn't understand, I mean look at all the Greek gods. I think they are all naked statues.

There was an empty barrel beside the toilet. I managed to go inside it and jumped out every time I heard footsteps. They say little amuses kids, but at least we were getting our kicks.

Simon came across and said, "Your pictures are ready for collecting, the ones with no shoes." He chuckled. I replied, "Go across and pick them up for us." He said, "No way, I have to pay money if I take them." I told him we didn't want them anyway. I said go and have a look; he quickly removed them and paid for them. He said, "I can't believe you had your dick out again, Ron. Friking unbelievable, you guys."

We never did go to Skegness. Two of the three Waterboys could make it, but the other was away on business, we would have loved to go on that trip, but it just wasn't to be.

Chapter 9

'Gan to see Selic'

I like to be different. When it comes to supporting football teams and traveling down to games, I consider it different. Everyone says you should support your local team, but Aberdeen FC didn't really appeal to me as the first time I went to the stadium as a neutral, I wondered how a team with 4000 fans could make more noise than the other 14000 (home side). That day I was watching Celtic V Aberdeen. The place was electric one minute and like a morgue the next. That particular day, Aberdeen beat Celtic, 4 goals to 1. Frank MacDougal scored all four, but the Celtic supporters made more noise!

How could this be? It intrigued me so much, I followed the away supporters to their buses parked on the beach, just to try and understand where there passion was coming from.

I told my brother the next game I want to go to is a Celtic game. He told me I would have to save my green final money (a sports paper that was issued every Saturday where I earned more for 1 day's work than the kids delivering papers every day at an ungodly hour in the morning before school).

It took me three months to save to go down to the game. My brother drove me down. I was 14 years old on the way down to Glasgow to see Celtic. Little did I know, this would turn out to be a love affair with a club that is close to every supporter's heart. The thing that amazed me the most about that day was, during the four-hour drive, we passed countless buses, and many from my home area! Buckie,

Aberdeen, Huntly, why didn't my hometown have a bus going down every week?

As me and my brother went to park our car, we were greeted a boy my age, saying he would look after our car! I was intrigued and asked him why he should look after our car. He said because if we didn't our stereo would disappear. I gave the young entrepreneur the money and went on our way, knowing our car would be safe.

I can't remember much about the game. It was against St. Mirren, not very appealing but what intrigued me more was the banter (the quick witted Glaswegian humor). I overheard many stories, not one dissimilar to the car story we had encountered. It went like this; the guy was asked the same question, if they wanted their car looked after. The owner replied, I have a big dog in the back of my car that will look after it. The young guy quick as anything asked if their dog put out fires! I was giggling away to myself, but it wasn't finished! He never gave the young lad any money, and the young guy never set fire to his car, but fed the dog some laxative and you can imagine the stench.

One of my first old firm games was during the early 80's when Celtic had some small connections with the IRA hunger strikers. I remember going to some games and you would see people with buckets and Balaclavas, saying 'money for the cause'. I was always curious about these connections, nothing that I condoned but certainly never supported. It's amazing what people's religious belief brings to football clubs and the heartbreak that comes along with it.

The songs that Celtic fans sing really have nothing to do with football and about 80% of the fans that sing these anthems really don't know what the songs are all about. One of these songs in particular was the 'Roll of Honor'. If you listen to the way this song is chanted at the matches and the tempo it has, it certainly adds to the atmosphere. The Roll of Honor is about a group of hunger strikers in the maze prison, a prison that housed terrorists, most of whom tried to commit treason towards the British government and the armed forces. The way I saw it, they were living in the dark ages and what's gone is gone, don't try to bring up your own children on the same mentality or we will never be rid of the hatred and rebellious nature and habits.

We had made or way to this particular old firm derby at Parkhead early, as we wanted to try and get into the Jungle. The Jungle, or Janfield road area, was where all the humor and Craic happened; this is where you got your Celtic education. I remember being in this end when Celtic destroyed Sporting Lisbon 5-0 and the late great Tommy Burns (Tommy Runs Tommy Turns Tommy Burns) had turned in one of his finest performances in a Celtic Jersey. I was with a friend during that game, and as we stood in the Celtic end beside the gate to the Jungle, pleading with the Polis to let us in the gate, they would only let in a few at a time, a bit concerned about the crush factor. Of course, this was all before the Hillsborough Disaster. I asked the Policeman if there was any chance of him opening the gates and letting us in. He ignored me at first. As the crowd grew behind me, I asked the question again. He turned round and pointed at a 3 inch gap at the bottom of the gates and said, "Could you crawl under there?" I said, "No way!" He replied, "Bobby Sands Could." Five guys behind me surged forward, foaming at the mouth and smelling of Buckfast, screaming and shouting obscenities at the Policeman. I laughed at what was just said and thought, to myself *no way is he opening the gates after that statement.*

For those who don't know, Bobby Sands was the man behind the hunger strikes, a very much a talismanic figure, but certainly not in my eyes.

One evening, which will remain in my mind for the rest of my life, was Friday May 13th, 1988. I was playing for my local side and I was through 1 v 1 with the keeper. I swung for the ball, then I felt slight contact from behind from the defender, enough to put me off balance, then I kicked the goalkeeper right on the pelvis. I was lying on the ground, my leg felt numb, the pain not quite set in yet. I heard the goalkeeper shouting and saw him rolling around in agony. The referee, whom I was familiar with, asked me to get up as he was booking me for such a challenge! I said, "Alasdair have you ever booked a player with a broken leg before?" He replied, "It's not you that's injured, look at the goalkeeper!"

I replied, "If you don't believe me, watch this." To this day, I don't know why I did it! I lifted my leg and holding on to the knee, and my lower leg folded it in half! "Now you fuckin believe me?" He replied, "Ron, stay there. I will get ambulance for you."

All I could think about was the next day I had arranged 18 tickets for the Scottish cup final, Celtic v Dundee Utd, centenary season. My friend came across and I said, "You can have my ticket."

The Doctor who delivered me as a baby came to me and said, "You will have to travel to Aberdeen, as we cannot perform the operation here!" When I arrived by ambulance it was around 10.30 pm. I lay there thinking my sporting career was over. I wouldn't be able to walk or run again. What about my job? I had just started part-time work back at the local swimming pool! Well, at least rehab would be smooth. The surgeon came and said to me, we will put a plaster from the top of your hip to the top of your toes. I went to the operating theatre at 1.40 am, around 7 hours since I broke my leg, I woke around 8am, still with the effects of the morphine running through my veins. I felt numbness in my leg. I put my hands underneath the covers and felt no plaster, I thought perhaps my leg was not broken; I could get out and meet the lads for the game! Then I lifted the covers and to my horror, I saw this pinned contraption sticking out of my leg, I yelled for the nurse, demanding to know what it was. She told me to go back to sleep, the doctor would explain at 12 pm, when he did his rounds. I asked, "Can I have some more morphine?" It was a cheeky smile that she could not resist. So she gave it to me.

The Doctor awaked me, he explained that this was a breakthrough in medicine and I was one of the first patients to be using this in the northeast of Scotland. I was a guinea pig. I wasn't sure if I liked this idea. He assured me that it had been tried and tested in Sweden, and everything was positive. I was only curious how it all worked and who would clean this contraption on my leg, as the sexy nurse would not come to my house every day and clean, that was sure. The nurse explained to me how to clean the five pins. "When you have to clean them, you remove the gauze first and pour disinfectant on the pins, wipe it dry, then add gauze and dressing." I looked at her and said, "There is no way I can do this." She replied, "If you don't, your leg will become infected and you might lose it." I guess that's all the warning I needed. I made sure

I cleaned them after that. After lunch, I slept, reminding the nurse to wake me up at 2.30 pm (30 minutes before KO). As I settled down to sleep, I thought of my mates, on their way to the match, having a few beers and laughing and joking. Here I was with a broken leg, unable to do a thing.

I was wakened by a soft voice and saw this angel-like figure over me. As she leaned over, I pulled her onto bed and tried to kiss her. Of course, I hadn't a clue what I was doing. She was shocked to say the least. I was more embarrassed than she was, though I suppose it was not the first time that had happened to her. As she wheeled me to the TV room, I looked around and thought; *there are people in here that have more problems than just a broken leg.* I started to watch football and was becoming more animated, people came past and asked, "What you watching son?" When I replied, I must have seemed to be the rudest person in the world. I was expected to think everyone knew Celtic were playing the Scottish Cup final in their centenary year, going for the double, after last week they won the league on the last day of the season, beating St Mirren, 5-0. My mood was becoming angrier and angrier and more agitated. I have never been a good loser! Show me a good loser and I will show you a loser, a great quote from the Liverpool legend, Bill Shankly. Then Dundee Utd scored. I almost kicked the TV from its stand. If it hadn't been for my bad leg, I would have. I thought back to the time when my mother was going to Bingo and she asked me to dig the back garden. I thought, *all right as long as I get to listen to the football on the brand new 'beat box'.* This was my mother's pride and joy, a present from her boyfriend, Ian! She agreed and I got the extension cable out and plugged it in and listened to the league cup semi-final, Celtic v Dundee Utd, the very team they were playing in their centenary cup year. I was 16 years old, digging my mother's garden, listening to the football, quite happy. The game went into extra time and then United scored shortly after the final whistle went. I was so angry I took the spade and smashed it over the beat box. There were pieces flying everywhere. Then I realized, *my god this is my mother's pride and joy she is going to go crazy*! When she returned, I tried to cover it up and, as she liked to listen to her country and western before she went to sleep, I knew it was a matter of time before she asked for it. I asked her if she wanted a cup of tea, trying to stall things even more, then as I was in the kitchen, she asked where her stereo player was. Silence. She went through to the back lobby and said, "What have you done?" Then she said, "I suppose Celtic got beat." She knew exactly how I would react to such thing! I had a long year saving to replace that stereo player, but never really learned my lesson.

The one thing about Celtic, you can never write them off. With 4 minutes to go and losing 1-0, the blonde playboy scored (Frank Macavenie) a goal getter, with a great turn of pace. I shouted and the nurse came running and asked if I was ok. I think when she saw the size of my grin, she knew the answer. I was feeling tired, I had to stay awake for extra-time, then in the second minute of injury-time, from a corner, the blond playboy struck again, with a 2 meter headed goal. I was ecstatic. If I could have jumped, I would have. I thought of my mates, jumping up and down and making the 360 mile round trip worth its while.

I went to bed with a smaller dose of morphine! I slept like a baby and all I wanted was to get out of the hospital. The doctor came round and asked me how I was feeling. As usual, I replied, "Good, when can I go home?" He asked the nurse to go and get the crutches and said if I could climb that stairs, I would be out this time tomorrow afternoon!"

I have always been determined, as I am stubborn, so hence to say, I climbed that stairs and was on my way home the very next day.

When I arrived home, all I could think of was getting up and down the hills of my town. Each day, I went further. The first day I went 100 meters, turned around and came back home, each day determined to get further than the last. By then end of the 12 weeks, I was walking 6k three times a week on my crutches. Many of my friends, would stop and ask if I wanted a lift and my reply was always no!

One of the worst things about rehab, as most people will vouch for, is the time it takes to get the muscle definition back. I thought I would never be able to run again! One day, during my rehab at the local swimming pool, my old manager noticed me. He asked if I come into his office after. He had something to talk to me about. When I spoke with him, I couldn't believe my ears. He was offering me a full-time position. I asked about an interview? He just said, "The job is yours, all you have to do is apply." On the day of the interview, there were three people before; they were all looking dressed for the part and ready to accept the position. When I went into the office, the first thing they said was, "When can you start?" I didn't even need an interview. So there was the start of a 17-year spell with Aberdeenshire council, of which I am grateful for all the courses and training I received under them, good and bad times. I have to admit; I didn't have too many sick days, which is a testimony of keeping yourself fit. If you do that, you keep the bed bugs away.

When given ultimatums in life, you either decide what's best or what's not, I chose the first.

I have been engaged to three women in my short life. This had been the only one that felt right. We had travelled the world together. 19 out of the 20 flights had been first class air travel. We were both working class. The only difference was she was a trolley dolly that worked for Virgin Atlantic. Of course, I wasn't allowed to say my first class tickets were £50. I met some very interesting people during flights, one time I was travelling to Las Vegas. It was a week before Xmas. I was sitting at the bar having a soft drink and I noticed a pretty average looking guy sitting opposite. Average meaning he wasn't the run of the mill typical business guy. I went over and struck up a conversation. I asked what his reason was to fly to Vegas just before the festive season and I asked what his occupation was. He told me he was a postman. I said, "Did you steal a couple of big checks in the post?" He replied that he had actually won 2.4 million pounds on the lottery, lucky bastard. He said the reason he needed to get away was he needed time to think about how he was going to share the money between his family, and he wanted to relax and enjoy Vegas for 5 days. Bloody scary place, that Vegas. 1st night he lost $10,000, 2nd he won $5000 and the 3rd he lost $15,000. Then he started to put things in perspective. He had lost the equivalent of 2 years' salary as a postman in just 3 days and that money was better spent amongst his family and friends.

2003 was the year that probably changed my direction on life. Having worked with the authority for 17 years, I was beginning to get bored. Should I stay or should I go, a great Clash song was playing in the workplace. Same people coming to use the facility day in and day out. I needed a challenge, so I spoke to my girlfriend and suggested that I move down to be with her. She seemed keen from the start, but I could tell she wasn't 100% behind the idea. It was around about the same time my beloved Glasgow Celtic were in the semifinal of the Uefa Cup and from the moment Henrik Larsson's scalfed shot against Boavista in the second leg of a tense Uefa Cup semi-final arched into the back of the net, my life was about to change.

I was ecstatic. I called my girlfriend and when she asked if I would go, my reply was yes, and her reply was if you go then the relationship is over. I was quite shocked to say the least. I didn't know what to say. I guess this was an easy way out for her, she said she couldn't trust me going to Spain on my own.

She rang me many times on the days leading to the Final and I rejected the calls …

"I didn't believe 50,000 fans would travel to Seville. That is madness, an exaggeration. I think a fair number will be around 4,000. We are talking about a final being played on a Wednesday, a day when people work."

Nearly 80,000 Celtic supporters descended into the small city. Hoops and sombreros were visible on every inch of tarmac; not just around the ground, but in every nook and cranny of the town.

Yet, in the aftermath of the game, Spanish police would make not even one arrest. Fifa would later award the Celtic support with a Fair Play award for the manner in which they turned out to support their team. This is why I support this great club, we are more than a football club.

The road to Seville was a flight from Aberdeen to London, a flight to Madrid and a drive to Seville. We arrived in Madrid and many Hoops fans were there, a Rangers fan approached me and he wished our team luck. I asked if he was a true Rangers fan and he said of course. I said if the shoes were on opposite feet I certainly wouldn't be wishing his team luck.

I remember my first old firm game as a 17 year old receiving a blow to the head from an elderly gent (Rangers fan) just because he recognized the colors tucked under my shirt or the time our car was scratched by a women's shoe as she spat on the windscreen. I'm sure the favors have been returned, but I choose to go to a match to watch it, not fight.

We drove all night and arrived in the morning the day before the game. The place was buzzing and the fans were amassing, some estimated 80,000 had made the journey. I spoke to a guy from San Francisco and he didn't even have a ticket. Many stories were similar. Only 35,000 tickets were available, I was one of the lucky ones; Stu and Kev didn't have tickets.

We had just parked our car outside this public park. Many supporters chose to park there. I remember a car pulling up outside a battered old escort, the driver looked zonked!

As he reached over to the passenger door and opened it, his mate fell out intoxicated. The driver said they had been sitting in a bar Monday evening and decided to drive to the game. He said his friend hadn't been sober since they left, I doubt if they had jobs to go back to, but this is the spur of the moment decision that makes you love this club.

We heard so many stories during this trip, such as guys selling all their house contents, just for the travel and experience.

Later that day, having arranged to meet a friend of mine for my ticket, I told Stu and Kev I wasn't drinking till I had the ticket in my hand. We were all kilted up and stood around at the meeting point. Thousands of fans milled around, creating a real party atmosphere. I went away for a piss and as I returned I felt this guy's hand go inside my sporran (front purse for the kilt). I grabbed his hand before he could grab my wallet. I looked at him and was going to put him in a headlock, but he wriggled away with his accomplice an attractive woman. I noticed she had a bag full of wallets and purses. I shouted and warned others as they disappeared amongst the thousands of fans. The press had warned the fans that hundreds of pickpockets had made their way from Barcelona to take advantage of the intoxicated Celtic fans.

The Uefa Cup final of 2003 was a tense, dramatic, and emotional affair. The heat was draining - in late May in the tranquil city of Seville there was a barrie heat.

With KO fast approaching, the atmosphere was building. Jose Murinhno's Porto were favorites, but we had Henrik Larsson one of the best all round players I have seen, pull on the Hoops jersey.

We made our way to the stadium. The guys made their way to one of many giant screens as I made the trek to the ground. I saw a crowd milling around a couple of guys. It was former Celts Andy Walker and Derek Whyte. It was great seeing this! I always maintain Celtics are more than a football club and once you witness that feeling, it's very difficult to let go.

As we approached the stadium, there were many Porto fans looking to make a fast buck, trying to sell tickets five times face value at 500€ and what I witnessed next was quite amusing. A group of Celtic fans surrounded the guy and took his tickets and handed them to ticketless Celtic fans. As I entered the Stadium, I couldn't believe the sea of green and white and the noise was deafening. If you ever have the chance to witness a European night at Celtic Park, you'll know what I'm talking about.

The locals were amazed at their green-and-white city and were joining in on the party atmosphere whenever and wherever possible. Celtic lost the Uefa Cup final in the second half of extra time after being reduced to ten men with the 102nd-minute ordering-off of Bobo Balde for a second caution.

It was the first time a Uefa Cup final was decided on the "silver goal" rule - Derlei converting after Rab Douglas had spilled a shot and Ulrik Laursen's despairing boot could not keep the ball out of the net.

Twice Celtic had pegged Porto back to get on level terms and if Larsson -whose ability was viewed with some skepticism by those out with Scotland due to where he chose to play his football - showcased his ability, it was there in the Uefa Cup final with two beautiful headers, the first of which marked his 200th goal for Celtic. He was named the Man of the Match - Deco must have run him close for it - but it was an accolade that did not register with him in the aftermath of the game.

He was quoted after the match: "I don't see anything positive about my performance in the final. Scoring two goals in a final doesn't mean anything if you lose. All I wanted was for Celtic to win the cup." Years later, I saw him score against Celtic for Barcelona after, basically moving from defender to defender and selecting the weakest link to convert his chance. He was a footballing genius and also had the utmost respect for the club he served seven glorious seasons with. Even after winning the coveted, he was quoted saying, "I would have swapped a lot of what I achieved just to win in Seville."

During the Final, Jose Mourinho, though, for all his perceived arrogance, was gracious enough to admit he had been part of something special. He said: "As a football game, Celtic-Porto in Seville was the most exciting football game I have ever been involved in. An unbelievable game. Every time I see Martin O'Neill I remember I was the lucky one that day. An incredible match. I've never seen such emotional people. It was unbelievable."

Seville ended in tears. But ultimately there was pride amidst the heartbreak, pleasure to take from the pain. But there was more heartache for me. After the match, I made my lone trek back to where the car was parked. That was a long walk and it was hard to take. I had mixed emotions about my ex-girlfriend, Celtic, just losing and of course my life, what direction was I going to take. When I arrived at the car Stu and Kev were already there. As I approached the car, I could see the back window had been smashed. I looked for my holdall, gone as if Paul Daniels had just been there. I thought, *shit, my passport, return ticket, and sentimental clothes are all stolen*. The night was going from bad to worse. The plan was to try and get some sleep and go and deal with things the next day. As I was lying next to the car in my sleeping bag, as the car was full of broken glass, so not possible to sleep inside it, I felt this scratching on my head. I was half asleep and I thought it was a cat. Then it ran across my face. It was a huge Rat; god knows how long it had been creeping around me. There was no way I was getting much sleep after that.

It was around 5.30am when I woke. I don't remember sleeping, but must have nodded of between rats. We made our way to the local police station. As we queued, we realized we weren't the only ones who had fallen victims to the car break-ins. I guess drunks were easy targets.

As the door opened and we all stumbled inside the police station, to report our loss, I wondered how I could travel without passport or flight ticket!

It's times like this when you realize the extent of it. This guy, around 75 years old from Glasgow wondered in, no money, no ID, and still intoxicated and all he said was he missed the bus, how could he get home. At least he was in good spirits.

The policeman, in broken English, said, I would have to go to the British Embassy, so they could issue an emergency document to allow me to travel. We drove there in a car with no back windows and we got some strange looks at the traffic lights. Approaching the Embassy, we saw many Celtic tops. I suspect we were all in the same boat. The shocking stats were, that almost 200 passports had been stolen that evening. I wonder how many underhand dealings have been involved with those passports.

The next incident was waiting to hand over my temporary passport at the Airport. The assistant asked me for my ticket, I explained to her it had been stolen along with my passport. She said, "Then you have to purchase a new one and it will be full price!"

Trying to remain calm, I said my name is surely in the system and manifest, why can't you just reissue a new one. She apologized and said it was just company policy.

I then said, "This is my first visit to Spain and I don't have a very good impression of your country; lost passport, lost ticket, and my team has just lost the Ueaf cup. Surely you can issue a low budget ticket." She said, "Ok sir that will be 120€." Luckily, I had my credit card, even though it had maxed out.

Arriving at Gatwick and waiting for my connecting flight, my thoughts moved to the ex-girlfriend. I called but there was no answer. I assumed she must have been on a flight!

The next day, I received a call early in the morning. We spoke and arranged to meet, but never did. I now realize things happen in your life for a reason. I guess we weren't meant to be.

It was summer 2004. Celtic had a North American tour. I bit the bullet and decided to go, an ideal opportunity to meet my old friend John a football (soccer) coach in the states. He had been married since '98.

Once you start to follow the hoops, it sort of enters your blood. The first game was Liverpool in Cincinnati. Celtic had a real makeshift team and played a really young side. There was around 5000 fans for this opening game. We lost 5-0, but the fans, as usual, were tremendous. Even in defeat they still were happy. This is the sole reason why

Celtic are asked to play in player testimonials all over the world. We will guarantee the support and the atmosphere.

The second match was in Philadelphia, a city made famous by Rocky. The club we played was the great Manchester Utd. Man Utd, Arsenal, and Celtic have the top selling season ticket books in the UK. Worldwide, Man utd just pip Celtic.

We were preparing for the match in one of the many Irish bars in Philly, the Wolftones were playing and 500 Celtic fans rocked the joint. There would be a fleet of yellow school buses escorting us to the game. Our bus was the lead and it was rocking. I asked the driver to stop at the Rocky stairs, the ones he ran up in the movies, the driver was a little hesitant at the start, but eventually he agreed.

When he stopped, 40 mad Celtic fans went running up the steps, shadow boxing and humming the Rocky tune. It was great fun, especially when the other buses did the same. The people of Philadelphia must have thought, "Who are these mad green and white hooped aliens?" As you know, football isn't all that popular in the states, and this is similar in Australia, America's baby brother when it comes to sense of humor, choose to call the beautiful game Soccer. Since when did you start to play football with a Soc?

This was a sellout, two of the biggest supported clubs in the world going head to head. Celtic was back to full strength and even managed to grab the first goal. The match ended 1-1 and we drove back to John's house. There must have been 20,000 Celtic fans and 15,000 Man utd, and the rest were neutral.

The final game was to be held in Toronto against As Roma. Travelling up to the game, we stopped in past Niagara Falls. A year later, I would see Victoria Falls, two wonders of the world.

During my visit to the states, I came across particular character that will remain in my memories forever, though not for the right reasons.

John, Erica (his wife), and myself were in a local bar on my first night. We were having a few quiet drinks and then the band stuck up a few notes. The tune sounded familiar; they were playing one of Celtics' favorite anthems and we both looked at each other, of course the words were different, but we could add the lyrics. During the break, we spoke with the band and asked if we could go and sing the Celtic song. They agreed. We started belting into song and the party atmosphere started. I glanced to the bar and this guy stood up and was singing along also, at the end of the song he shouted, sing *The Man behind the Wire*. This was a serious political song, a song from the troubles and definitely has views towards the I.R.A

After the song we went to the bar and met this flame haired Irish immigrant. His name was Tommy Maloe and he proceeded to tell us his life story. Complete strangers, we were, but he must have thought we were of the same cause. As the evening drew to a close, Tommy suggested we go for some more drinks at a local bar he knew. Erica looked at John as if to say, if you go then all hell will break loose when you return. So John declined the offer. I was never one to back down. I mean, what could possibly go wrong? As soon as I stepped into his pick-up truck, I thought, what the hell? He asked me to get his cigarettes from the glove department, as I opened it, he said don't

worry about the gun, that's in case we get into trouble.
W.T.F

We arrived at this bar, which could only be described as something from the Wild West, chicks with teeth missing, guys with teeth like rows of condemned houses. I stood at the bar and ordered two beers. People kept staring at me, perhaps because I was normal looking. Tommy approached the bar after greeting everyone like a movie star, I guess it was his local. It was then that something weird happened, Tommy accidentally stood on a guy's foot. The guy says, "What hell are you doing man, watch the fuck where you're going!" I thought, *give it a rest, it was an accident, these people made a big deal out of everything*. Tommy apologized and the situation was defused.

It was then Tommy spotted a couple sitting in the corner. He told me to hang back for a minute while he went across and talked to these guys. He'd come back soon. He seemed to be gone for a long time. Girls were coming up to me and asking me all sorts of shit. I was polite and thought this wasn't a place to assert my humor. When it comes to humor, sometimes it goes too far above people's heads and they can't take it and usually ends with trouble. Then my new friend, Tommy, appears back on the scene. He said, "I am going to be gone for an hour maximum, you will be alright here, don't worry man, you will be fine." I nodded. 'Fine by me'.

The karaoke was warming up. All the would-be Johnny Cash's had been up, the heavy rockers had been up, and now it was time for the Righteous Brothers, *You've Lost That Loving Feeling*. I certainly had, looking around the bar, even if I was intoxicated and had my finest beer goggles on, I wouldn't have selected anyone from this bar. Let's just say you definitely wouldn't take them home to your mother. The hours passed and still no sign of Tommy. I was getting worried, I had no hand phone, nor did I know the way home and if I didn't turn up, Erica and John would have been worried.

Then I breathed a sigh of relief as Tommy walked through the door and said, "Ok man, I will take you home." He was busy telling me of his sexual conquest he had just had with this women. She was there with her brother and he had known her for about six months. She used to go to the bar quite a lot but he hadn't seen her for a while. About two months ago her husband had been shot and killed in that very bar. *Great*, I thought, *and he left me in this bar knowing. Welcome to America.*

While driving home, he jammed his brakes on, skidded to a halt, and reversed back. He saw this old women walking down the adjoining street. He drove up to her, but realized it wasn't his friend's mother. He said she normally goes walking about in the early hours of the morning and said if he saw her he promised to take her home. As we drove off, he spotted a colored guy talking to a friend through the passenger window of this car. Tommy said, "Ron, do you like Blacks?" I said, "I am Scottish and have no problem with race or color, we just get on with our lives. As long as they don't bother me, I have nothing against them."

He said, "I hate them." He drove straight towards the guy. I thought, *Oh shit, this is going to be a homicide case I'm involved with.* He was calling my bluff, so I just played it cool and he pulled away at the last minute. Then I thought, *get me the fuck back to John's house.*

That evening was certainly an eye opener to America and some of the characters. We made fun of that to Erica during my visit and said I was going to call Tommy to arrange a night out. You always meet wonderful characters at the football and were always guaranteed a laugh, whether being at home matches or away ones.

The last story I will tell you about Celtic, involved a former player and manager of the club, the great Neil Lennon (a fiery headed Irish Man). He was a Celtic man through and through, a legend in his own right and a player you certainly wanted on your team. He wasn't the quickest player and rarely gave the ball away, but as a defensive holding player, he was one of the best.

We had been to a European game the previous evening and had no time to go to the club superstore, so the next day we decided to buy some souvenirs, as the next day was always quiet. As we left the store, I spotted Neil in his car. We had just entered our car, and I said to my mate, "Let's follow him." We must have only driven 200 meters and Lennon stopped outside the local bookies. We parked up and went in. At the time, I had this exploding pen and I told my mate I was going to ask Lennon for his autograph and ask him to sign it with my pen. My mate said, "Ron, you can't do that," and smiled. I guess he already knew I would carry out the prank. I approached Neil and asked for his autograph, he opened the pen and it gave out this almighty bang. Everyone looked round as the pen was hurled across the bookies and Lennon said in his best Northern Irish accent, "Fuck sake, I wasn't expecting that." Around this time he had been receiving death threats from a rival club's supporters; there must have been all sorts of things going through his mind as the pen exploded.

Chapter 10

Life Changing Experience Training for Africa!

November 2004 was when I decided to bite the bullet and move away from the town that gave me so much pleasure and life lessons…

Development instructor

I will always remember my first day at Winestead, getting picked up by Karen and Rolf. They were driving me to the camp, asking me: do you drink, smoke, or have a girlfriend? Why are you here? It was like the Gestapo. Driving into the grounds on a cold, wet, and miserable autumn evening, the first thing I saw was a football pitch. I thought, *not so bad*. I asked if there was a gym. They told me there was. "I can see you are quite fit and like sport, you will have a single room as you have paid more on this course than anyone else. So you shouldn't have a problem getting to sleep, house rules, no women on site, you can do what you want off site, but no women in the room or alcohol, you wouldn't be the first person to be kicked off, if this was to happen!"

Dinner was between 5pm and 7.30pm. They told me they would see me in the mess, get familiar with the site, everyone was friendly, there were many nationalities.

As I walked to the room, I saw a few people. They were walking like zombies, smoking roll ups, I tried to speak and all I got was a grunt. I asked this girl, Olga, from Hungary if she liked here and in her best broken English, she said, "Its ok but you have to be careful, don't get involved too much with the parties and stay away from certain people." I thought to myself, as I opened the door to my room, *why did I pay $5000 of my own hard earned cash for this?* It was like being a poor student. I lay on my bed and decided, what the hell? I would focus and be disciplined enough not to drink. I wasn't sure about having a girl in my room. Having seen what was on offer, I thought maybe no.

When I was walking to the mess, I saw everyone herding in like cattle and like clockwork. I guess if you weren't there on time you missed out. That was the first thing I learned and as I didn't have to do the hard labor of some of these eastern Europeans, who had come here to work like dogs to earn their money for their trip to Africa. I had already paid half and would have to fundraise to do the rest, shouldn't be a problem.

I sat beside these three Hungarian guys and they seemed really funny. They could speak good English, but I guess that was a way out of the country. After they showed me around, I went to the gym and said, "It's not the best, but we can do a class or two here." They said, "Do you teach?" I replied, just a little!

The next day in the mess, I was introduced to the school. There was 40 DI's all were being groomed to go all over Africa. When I saw the principal talking, I was quite amazed to see so many people switch off and one of the Hungarians made a joke. She took it well. I guess he was the school clown. Well there was a challenge for me!

The more time I spent at the school, the more I thought it was more of an institute. When you went to town, people would look at you and say, "Are you from Winestead?" As if you were inhuman. I tried to go into town on my own and not take the school bus. I was getting friendlier with one of the girls and pretty soon; I was sneaking into her room and she into mine. It was quite easy to do, as long as there was no fighting you could get away with pretty much everything! I never touched a drop of alcohol the whole time I was there, I was proud of that. To this day I can easily do without alcohol, there was no way I was going to go down the route of my father!

It was coming up to the first fundraising day and everyone was getting excited about getting out. You could go out every month and fundraise for 10 days, people would come home; some with no money, some with their target. I was advised to go local as it was my first one, so off I went every day and stood on the corner waiting for someone to buy my magazine, a bit like a big issue seller in Glasgow or any other town in the UK. The first day I made 10GBP for 8 hours of work, slave labor. I was making more picking tatties when I was 15. This was a hard sell.

 During those dark days of Fundraising, I decided my next trip would be Sheffield; off I went on the National Express (Bus). I selected a place just opposite Marks and Spencer's. I was wearing my kilt; it was always a good conversation starter. I seemed to recognize two people walking towards me and I was star struck. One was Kenny Daglish (my boyhood hero) and the other was Graeme Souness (Scourge of Celtic in the early, 90's and was sorely responsible for the demise of the Rangers, along with David Murray). Kenny spoke first and asked why a Scotsman was standing alone in a street in Sheffield? I told him my pitch and said he was my childhood hero when he played for the hoops. Souness walked away and said, "Come on Kenny, we will be late." They had come to Sheffield for Phil Neal's funeral. Kenny gave me a 5GBP, Souness gave nothing. I shouted, "Hey Graeme!" They both looked back. I said, "Once a Hun, always a Hun." I could see Kenny's shoulders moving; at least he knew what I meant.

The most successful day I had fundraising was in Scotland. You may find this hard to believe, but it was. The scots are renowned for being tight. They say two Scotsmen fighting over a penny invented copper wire. I went to visit a friend of mine, Fiona. She was a music teacher in Nairn (the fastest town in Scotland). She is the principal of music and doing really well for herself, recently she received an OBE. On this particular fundraising day, I happened to be in the right place at the right time. It was 'comic relief day' a day on which they fundraise for Africa. I bought a red nose and a bucket and I set off with my magazines. Within 2 hours I had collected over 120GBP, normally it would take one week to raise this. I had lunch and raised another 100GBP. Then I took the rest of the week off and did some sightseeing and prepared to go back to Hull. When I told the fellow DI's they were shocked and amazed by the generosity of the Scots.

Being at the school was certainly an experience; many of the DI's complained about how they were treated and the conditions. I just said, "Where we are going, do you think the conditions will be much better?" I hate people who complain about shit, just get on with the task in hand, get it done, you will encounter many obstacles in life, if you don't you won't learn.

Malawi

After deciding Malawi was my destination, I decided to
take one last trip home, I received some press in the local
newspaper and the doctor who delivered me gave me a
small donation. A local chemist gave me some medical
supplies, some for my own personal use and some for
emergencies in deepest darkest Africa. I also received an
interesting phone call from this 88year old lady, whom I
agreed to meet in her house. She told me a heartwarming
story about her sister Elspeth Mandell, who had worked as
a Nurse in Malawi and died from Malaria. She was working
in a place called Eqwindene which was a small town to the
north of Malawi. I promised her I would go there for my
investigation period and to see if the hospital still
remembered her. She also gave me a small donation,
which was very nice of her and out of respect, I fulfilled my
promise.

I remember thinking as I boarded the plane to Kenya, with
8 DI's, what sort of life changing experiences lay ahead of
me? Little did I know how much it would affect my life in
so many ways. Upon arriving in Kenya, we had a few hours
to kill. We couldn't leave the airport, as we needed a visa,
so we just walked around and waited for our flight
connection. I remember flying over Lake Malawi that very
morning and looking at its vastness and thinking, what a
beautiful country. I understand why Dr. David Livingstone
had fallen in love with the place. As we flew into the
Airport, Lillongwe, we were greeted by the Team of NGO's
welcoming us to the warm heart of Africa. The reason
Malawi is called this, it's because it has never had any civil
war, yet countries that have surround it seem to always be
in conflict. My country manager was part Malawian, part
Zimbabwean. He was a softly spoken man who reminded

me of a well-educated English gent. I knew in some way, shape, or form we would disagree with each other.

I personally wanted to make this as big an adventure as I could and wanted to do as much as I could for the community. I couldn't understand people who put all the time and effort into getting there and going half arsed. It has never been my way. I was assigned a project in a small town called Balagombe, it was around one and a half hours from Lilongwe, by any means. I remember being driven in Martin's 4X4 truck to the town and thinking, *is this it*? No electricity, no running water, a maternity clinic that supplied 50,000 people, and a generator that never worked. Where did all the NGO funding go? I was shown to my house. I had a look around; bed, table, kitchen, no stove, and cook with Charcoal. How would I survive for 7 months in this environment? The one thing that shocked me the most was the amount of children wandering around aimlessly in the village and the adults sitting around doing jack shit (men). Where were the other DI's? I waited, and around 4 pm, Andy and Veronica walked into the house. I introduced myself and they started to tell me about life as a DI. Andy said, "Let's go for a walk, Ron, I need to go and get some water." We each took a bucket and as we left the house, a flock of children followed us. They were singing, dancing, and being really happy, shouting, "Hey, Azungu." That meant white man. Andy seemed to be quite fluent in the language and had a good rapport with the kids. He said he worked in and around the schools and he had set up a youth group, where the teenagers could put across the message of HIV (Aids) which 33% of the population were infected with. He was a great musician and would write songs and the children would go around nearby villages explaining about how not to catch this terrible disease.

When we arrived back, Veronica had already started to prepare dinner; some soya, vegetable, and Nisma (dough type porridge made from maize flour) that had no nutritional value whatsoever. If this were to be my staple diet for the next 6 months, then I would be in trouble, internally. I tried to eat this only twice a week and live mainly on the sweet bread and peanut butter I purchased from the city I went to twice a week for my sanity to send emails, communicate with friends on messenger, and just to let everyone know I was alright.

The next evening I decided to take a walk around the village. I came across a game of football and stood and watched, I was amazed at there lack of tactics, Kick the ball upfront and hope for the best, for those who know anything about football there, formation was 4-1-5.

After the training I spoke to one of the players and told of them I was the new DI, I jokingly said do you want me to coach the team. He was jumping around with excitement, why did I open my big mouth.

What I did learn from coaching these guys was how much they loved their sport. One particular guy was called Soldier. He was a regular at training and was an extremely hard defender, not many players could get past him. He was like a rock at training. But what I was confused by was his lack of interest to play on the weekends! he was never there. I often said, "Where is soldier? Why did he not show up?" They said he was always working with his uncle in his maize field and couldn't play on the weekend. Later, I was going to find out the truth why Soldier never played on the weekend.

We were busy training for the competition, and as it was fast approaching I said to my guys, excitedly, "Who are we playing?" They had been to around three meetings and still had no answer. That's the one thing that frustrated me about Malawi, the speed that things would not get done, unless you followed up yourself. It was one of the laziest countries I have visited, but that's how they roll, no hurry no stress.

We finally had the news and they showed me the fixture list. We had four in our league and the first three fixtures were away from home. I said, "Why do we have to travel away?" Well, it turned out last year they also played some of these teams and they all, played at our ground, so it turned out we had to play away to return the favor. I had the system of which we played in my head and, of course, I knew this would confuse the opposition, as they had never played formations before. We met on Saturday morning, and I asked the guys how far it was to the field. They told me, not far boss. The thing about Africa is some kids walk 6k to school, so not far is around 6k. We walked about 10k and arrived at the pitch. The first thing I noticed was the amount of people. There must have been 1,500 supporters. We had around 50, which was a great effort. We started to play and our formation was going ok, but we were caught in the counter and we were down 1-0. It was half time and I was giving them a team talk. I said, "Don't worry too much, just stick to the plan and it will be alright." We ended up drawing the game 1-1. I asked when the next game is, they said tomorrow. I asked how far and again they replied, not far boss!

The next day, we met outside the school and we trekked another 7k and again there was a very big crowd. We won that game 4-0 and we had a good chance of making the semifinals. All we needed was 2 points from 2 games and one game was at home against a team that had never won a game in 2 years. We drew on the Saturday and the following week at home we knew we had qualified, so there was not too much pressure, but this was a home game. I was to realize different.

It was great to have a home game. I was excited, especially as we didn't need to walk too far. The game started at a frantic pace and pretty soon the home crowd was getting on our backs and the players back's also. We weren't sticking to the formation, the players were running around aimlessly, and they had lost their shape. I couldn't understand, the opposition was very average and we should have been well on top. It was around 10 minutes before the end of the half and bang, we were down 1-0. I couldn't believe it, the crowd was booing and shouting at the players. We managed to score just before half time, so we went in all square. I let the guys go into the changing room first (classroom) and then I was going to give them the hairdryer treatment. I took the ball and walked into the classroom. All the kids were looking through the window. I think they knew I was going to go crazy. The first thing I asked was, what the hell was going on and why weren't they sticking to the formation. They were silent. I took the ball and volleyed it just above one of the player's head and asked if they wanted to win the match or what! Of course boss, they said. I said, "Why are you playing like shit then?" They said the fans did not like the way they were playing, they wanted us to go and play the old way."

I replied, "Playing the old way didn't get you to where you are today, did it?"

We went out and won the game 3-1, playing the new way. I was carried down the street like a celebrity. I am pretty sure I could have married anyone that evening, not that I wanted to as HIV Aids was at 30% for the Village, might as well put a gun to you're head.

At training on Thursday I told a soldier we wanted him to play. He replied, "Maybe." That means no in Africa. This game was when I realized that cheating is a way of life and even if you were to give someone advice, it would make no difference.

We walked 7k to the field. We hadn't played this team before; I was sussing them out before the warm up. They couldn't understand our warm up; short passing, control, give and go. Man v Man we were much better than them. I thought it would be a walk in the park, there were around 2000 fans lining the pitch. It was difficult to see the line. After 5 minutes, I could see the way the match was going. The ref was a homer (not a neutral), we had a chance mid-way through the first half. Our guy was through 1 v 1 he scored and the ref gave offside. I couldn't believe he was a mile onside, our fans were going crazy - they wanted to fight! 10 minutes before the end of the half our best player went in a challenge and the guy was rolling around in agony. Our best player was red carded, from the resulting free kick they scored and just before half time; we played an offside trap and waited for the ref to blow. The guy ran through and scored 2-0, at least 10 yards offside.

At half time, our supporters surrounded the ref. They would have killed him if I hadn't stepped in. I said to him, "You have made some really bad decisions in this game so far." He agreed and I said, "You need to even it up or I won't be responsible for my supporters." I told the players to hold their heads up and just play their best. They were against a twelve man and we have very little chance, though. We lost another goal at the start of the second half and we scored two minutes to go. What I saw next was like something out of Benny Hill. Upon the final whistle, the ref blew and then he ran like a bat out of hell, through the village, as he knew our lynch mob was out to get him. I would have done the same, but then again I would never have made the decisions he had. I found out after the game that the prize for the tournament was the equivalent of one year's salary to each player and the village chief got 100 dollars, which was double what the player received.

It was during one of my visits into town, something caught my eye, as I glanced over at a billboard it read 'fixtures for the world cup qualifiers,' Malwai V Botswana.

I had a plan. I knew none of the players had been out of the village; so I decided to take these players to watch this game, pay for everything. I worked it out it - would cost me around $200, transport, match entry, and some food and beers, for 15 people. Why not? But I have always maintained you have to work for it to earn it. The next training session, with around 20 people there, I was to make the announcement. There are 20 training sessions and 4 matches, from now until the WCQ game, if you attend all, then you will have a chance of going to this game, if you miss one then you might not get to the match. The players were all ecstatic, jumping up and down. I mean, they were going to see their heroes, players that they watched only crowded around a TV set, which was powered by a car battery and the signal wasn't even that great. During the build up to the game, I could see the guys who were eager to go and even if they were sick they would come to watch the training, I think back and wondered if they were sick with the disease, are they still alive today.

I had 17 players, all with 100% attendance. It came down to drawing straws and a toss of a coin. I felt really sorry for the two who never went, but I would say it was God's wish and they could understand that. I had paid for the transport and we were all waiting for the bus to show, we had guys frantically calling the driver wanting to know where he was. Perhaps he got lost in the bush. I just hoped the bus would show up. I didn't want to let the team down. As I looked in the distance and the red dust was flying up, I knew this was some form of transport. I could see the bus lights and I felt a warm glow inside my body. Finally, we were on our way, 500km drive to watch Malawi. A 60,000 sellout, would I be the only white person in the crowd?

We arrived two hours before kick-off. I had many people approaching me and asking for my autograph. I felt like a celebrity, but I had 15 team members protecting me, I asked the bus driver if he wanted to come to the game also. Yes, of course, boss. Why would he drive all this way and not want to go also? As I made my way into the stadium, I heard a great crescendo of noise coming from the crowd, as the players came out for the warm up. I said to the players, "I want you to watch a player in each team for the first 10 minutes. A player that plays in your position. You will learn more from their movement and understand how I would like you to play. Watch for 10 minutes and then enjoy the game." I knew they would be playing like this, as they were managed by two European coaches. I asked the guys what formation Malawi was playing, they replied 4-4-2. Botswana? 4-3-3. Why you think this, I asked. I think Botswana is here to win, they replied. Botswana won the game 3-1 and from then I had the respect as a coach from the players and we played formations, from then on in as they understood.

On the journey home, we stopped outside this local bar and the guys were singing and dancing and saying how it was the best day of their lives. We were just about to leave when a fight broke out. It took a lot to provoke a Malawian, so it must have been serious. As we all got into the bus, one of the guys said the man in the bar insulted me and they were just sorting the issue out. I guess I was like a father figure to these guys. I think I would have done the same thing if I were in their shoes.

We were beginning to play less and less games, as we were approaching the rainy season and it was during a particular walk home I was to find out why Soldier would only train with the team and not play games on the weekend.

Gule Wamkulu (ghoul e Van Cool)

One day, I was walking home from the town. I loved doing this, just observing the day to day life of a Malawian, kids walking home from school singing and dancing, when they were going home to parents who were crippled with this horrible disease that swept across the warm heart of Africa. As I rounded a corner, I could hear drums beating from the village, I was about to get the shock of my life.

Out from behind a hut, I saw this person dressed in a peculiar manner and was headed right towards me with spear in hand, I could see his movements were to the beat of the drum. He was in front of me dancing, my heart was skipping a beat, I had no clue what to do, and then a young kid popped up and said, "Give him some Kwaccha." (Money) So I gave him money and he went back into the village. I was curious to what this was and I asked one of the guys and they explained, these Gule Wamkulu are invited to dance at ceremonies, weddings, funerals, and major events. They are invited to ward off spirits and give good luck to the ceremonies and help talk to the people who have passed away. I was intrigued; I wondered why their identity was hidden and why it was such a secret. I had to find out more.

At the next football training session, I spoke to nearly all of the players and was informed there was a major ceremony at our village this coming weekend, many Gule Wamkulu would come from other villages to take part in this yearly event. I asked if I could attend, they said of course, the event was for everyone. The ceremony started at 12 pm and carried right on until dark. I was amazed at the choreography and the way these people moved and the children would be really frightened if any of these figures came close to them. One team of three caught my eye. They were amazing the drummers, it seemed as if they were in a trance and the movement of the guys was great. I was sitting beside one of the football team members, they were all drunk, they had been drinking Cumbuku (maize alcohol) all day. One of the guys said, "You know the guy in the middle." I said, "How do you work that out, I can't even see his face because of mask." He told me it was Soldier!

The guy who had spoken seemed really worried, because he had just revealed a Gule Wamkulu identity, seemingly it was bad luck to do this, as these people are like gods and to become one is such a privilege and an honor.

I promised not to say a thing, but I had a plan! I asked the captain of the soccer team if he could ask me to meet these guys in secret, as I wanted to learn a little bit more about the culture. I said in return, I would give them some money and would buy a new ceremony dress for them, which I would like to design. I knew this was going to be a long shot, but as we know, there's a price for everything.

On the evening they came to my house it was very dark, of course there was no lighting in the village. People moved around in the shadows, they came to the house one by one, so not to reveal too much. The questions and answers below are exactly what were discussed.

How long have you been a Gule Wamkulu? / We have been a team for 5 years.

What do you have to do to become one? / Our father or uncles have been one also and we are the chosen family to become one.

What happens before the ceremony? / We are basically given the freedom of the village, we can select women in the village, before and after the ceremony, and we have sex with them. It's like an honor for the family or husband if your wife is chosen.

How much do you earn from this? / Basically we can earn in two days what a local can earn in one month.

Where do you practice your routines and when? / We practice at the graveyards; we tend to practice more when there is a major event, like every night.

Why do you practice at the graveyards? / We do this so we get the energy from the spirits of the dead.

Can I come to watch you dance one evening? / Yes, sure you can you can come tomorrow.

I went to see them dance. They seemed to be in a trance and this is where they got their power. I had no arguments of what they did, I respected their beliefs. What I was more concerned about was the fact that they were sleeping with so many infected women and they were passing on the disease. I wonder if any of them are still alive today.

I was staying a few weeks at the Nearby Orphanage

So I usually always head back to our village, but today I was fortunate because my accommodation was not in the house, but in a nearby orphanage, which functioned as a school as well. The students were crossing from 6 a.m. until 4 p.m. every day. There, we had no electricity or running water. The property of the orphanage was huge; it had its own vegetable garden.

On evenings, when everything was quiet, I sat out on the porch, listening to the night sounds, and watching the orphans, still awake, but preparing to go to bed, and thought about their future when the orphanage would close or they reached the age when they had to go. The leader of the orphanage had told me that an elderly man from the USA, who was really old, more than 70 years, supported the orphanage. The leader said he couldn't imagine what would happen if the man wasn't there anymore; how would they manage themselves? He showed me their monthly budget; it was really a lot of money.

As I've mentioned before, the road there was horrible. The nearest main road, where I could travel by bus, was a two-hour walk from there. If I wanted to go to shop in the city or the market, it almost took a whole day if I couldn't find a car that took me at least to the main road. The car of the dormitory was always occupied; it was very rare when they could take me or bring me back. Fortunately, I had more friends owning a car by then, so when they saw me walking down the road, they stopped and picked me up. The dormitory was one hour away on foot. I couldn't dine there because I would have to walk home alone at night, which was not recommended for anybody around there. It was a better solution, if I cooked for myself, or dined at the kitchen of the orphanage. Their life was not so varying; they eat nsima (maize porridge) with vegetables almost every day, with meat on the weekends.

I can cook rice, pasta, potato, and eggs for myself with vegetables, which I can buy at the market. I rarely shopped in the city, because the imported food was very expensive. I usually hurried home at 4 o'clock, packed up to the neck, so I could start my two-hour walk home and get home before dusk, if no one picked me up. Many times, total strangers stopped for me and asked where I was headed, what they could help me with. And the children would run after me, screaming "azungu bye" (azungu – white person)! They were so happy when I stopped to shake their hands.

If I was in a bad mood, or I felt lonely, it was enough if I went to walk 1-2 hours. I would cheer up for sure after that.In Malawi, although time passes very fast, everything works slowly.

If I have an arrangement with somebody and something happens, so he cannot come, but he doesn't inform me sometimes I wait unnecessary hours while I could do something else. I have learned a lot of patience and tolerance here.

Every single day like this is a great challenge for me. But this is why life here is wonderful; I don't have a clue what will happen in the next hour or minute. I really enjoy the challenges, the new people, and the totally different culture. The women wear skirts; this is tradition here, you can't see a woman in trousers anywhere. Many are walking down the street, singing without any reason or music, almost dancing. Those who are walking together or talking, often do that holding hands. Like this, you can see from far away who are going together. For me, it is very strange when I see two men walking hand-in-hand, although they are just talking. Many times, they try and hold my hand, but it's not the done thing in Scotland (you would be called a big poof/Jessie). Many of the houses don't have running water or a drilled well. The women bring home the buckets of water or other times the firewood, balancing these on their heads. I've tried this also, but I could not walk even one meter, I couldn't balance a thing, everything just collapsed. Slowly but steadily, I'm getting used to the life here. I've made many friends and new relationships. I like living here and time passes very fast. I am not looking forward to the day when I have to leave Malawi and go back to Scotland.

Discipline is the Key

I have always had the same philosophy, nothing in life comes easy. You have to go out and earn it; God won't help and it doesn't matter how much you pray, it will never come your way. There were around ten religions in this town and everyone followed one and if they had a problem with the one they followed, they just joined another. I was getting more and more frustrated with the way things were going and nothing seemed to move, unless you had money, of course, but to volunteer for something to help the community, they still held their hand out. Nearly every Sunday, I would go for a walk and sit beside the soccer field and listen to the Africans singing in their churches, coming out dressed with their best clothes on and looking at me and wondering why I was not at a church or mosque.

Many priests, imams, and Vicars, asking me to go to their congregations, approached me. I said, "For whose benefit?!" If I went along, all they would say I belong to their faith or religion. I wasn't prepared to do that for there own personal bragging rights. I used to ask people why they changed religion, I found out later, if you did something wrong in the community, like steal or beat your wife or cause a fight etc. etc., you were allowed a second chance in another church. Have you ever heard so much bullshit in your life? I have never believed in any God and never will. I married a Muslim woman for love and not for the God she believed in, why should this be forced on you, because you have not been brainwashed as a kid? Believe in who you are and not what you believe in what will be!.

The one thing I enjoy about travelling is finding out about cultures and beliefs. It's amazing what people believe in and follow. During my spell in Malawi, I was to have my eyes opened into a variety of things, like superstitions and witchcraft.

There was a woman in the village and she was married to the agricultural minister for the area. The husband was away on business regularly. They had two children and they were both a private school. I guess she was bored and lonely, she had many boyfriends coming and going in her house and it was a matter of time before the trigger was pulled (she would become infected). She never took any precautions, I mean why would she? The day before her funeral, there was an accident on the main road to her village. It just so happened to be where they had just built the road next to the cemetery. People were saying they couldn't travel on this road, as the spirits were angry, they have been upset because you built the road there. A three-hour journey to her village, now suddenly became a five-hour one, because people would detour the road, believing if they travelled past in that direction, the spirits again would be upset. I mean, WTF?
I have heard some horror stories, if this disease infects you. Why are people so uneducated and don't understand the difference between right and wrong? Why would the witch doctor tell you to do such a ghastly thing? Some believed if the virus infected you, the only way you could get rid of this was to have sex with a newborn baby, who would result in the death of the child, but you would be free of the virus. How can people think this way?

Some of the others were not so graphic, we would go regularly to the clinic to help and assist with the voluntary, testing and counseling to these people. Sometimes it was too late, and you just couldn't change beliefs. We used to tell them how to prevent the disease from spreading. We used to hand out free condoms and use the banana as an example, saying this was the way to prevent the disease from spreading. We would visit them in their homes and see bananas with condoms, nailed to the front door; we would ask what's that for? They explained, you told us if we did this we would not become infected. It's so frustrating when this sort of information gets lost in translation.

There was one occasion when I saw one of the players used the elastic band on the condom, to tie up his socks during training. It so happened to be Solider. I thought to myself, *he is the one person that should be having protected sex.*

The sex subject in Malawi is very much taboo. Men and women are very rarely are seen in public showing their affection to each other. They tend to show behind closed doors or at the gable end of houses, hidden in the shadows. I would often speak to some of the girls during the day and they would be embarrassed and would almost run away from a conversation. People just don't socialize or show their feelings, and they almost would lead you to believe that sex never happened.

We had a women come to the house on a regular basis to have some food, she had learning difficulties and had a baby strapped to her back. We used to give the poor, malnourished child some milk and bread and, occasionally, some eggs. I don't know if she had a home, we saw them on a regular basis. One day I spoke with Soldier and he said this was her fourth child, and the same thing happens to all. I was confused. *Were they taken from her when they reached a certain age? Were they being fostered?* Soldier told me they all die and usually she would carry them on her back for a few days after, not realizing what had happened to her baby. Two weeks after, this is exactly what happened. A terrible tragedy. What chance did the baby have?

Certain people use religion as power, especially in a poor community. I have nothing against religion, I just don't understand it and the subject is better left alone. The village had just been introduced the Muslim faith and what they did was they pumped lots of money into the community and of course the organizers get rich and the poor remain poor in the short term. They approached us and gave us a donation; even though it was small we put it to good use by buying some clothes and toys to give to the orphans and the really poor.

I warned Veronica it would be better going to people's house individually and distributing it, but she suggested we had a stall at the event. I did warn her. Everything was going smooth and in an orderly manner, then kids started to come in twice, jumping the queue, I noticed this straight away. I suggested 'we need to pull the plug on this before it escalates and becomes a riot'. I am glad she listened.

A few days later, I was shocked when she was setting up a table in the garden; I asked her what the purpose was! She said, I have two girls helping me I am going to distribute the remainder of the clothes in the garden after school. I asked if she was crazy!! She asked me to back off and basically mind my own business. When people only work with children and socialize with kids only, then the mentality changes. I was about to step in and help her. She had her views, I only hoped there would be no repercussions. The time was approaching and the plan seemed to be working, one girl controlling a queue outside the door, Veronica sitting and assisting with the clothes handover. Then the teenagers started to gather and look over our wall and into the garden. I was observing from the porch after about 15 minutes, it started to get really vocal. You could see the look of anxiety on Veronica's face. Then *bang* the gate was kicked in and it was like a stampede in the Serengeti. Within one minute, everything was taken and Veronica lay trampled to the ground, holding a six-month-old baby. She started screaming at me, why didn't you help? Have you no feelings of remorse? I made sure everyone was all right and I went inside.

The three girls came in and were crying, I gave them a hug and said, "Don't worry we know who most of the children are, why don't we go round to their houses and get the clothes back and we can distribute them to the orphans tomorrow, individually." I think finally Veronica saw some sense.

I went to retrieve some of the clothes from the houses and we actually retrieved around 85%, so that was good. We would go the next day and retrieve the rest. The next morning the two girls came to our house and said they had to go and see the village chief about yesterday. They returned and said they had been fined 500 kwacha (about one week salary) and a chicken (about one week salary). I said don't worry; I will pay your fines. The reason for the fine was they had to ask the village chief's permission first before they had to visit the house. Have you ever heard so much bullshit?

A little money goes a long way.

As my investigation period was coming to an end, I decided to leave a footprint in the village. I asked some villagers, "What has been set up before and why has it fallen by the wayside?" They said when the DI's leave, the funding stops and so do the projects. I was particularly interested in this small derelict shop in the village. I asked one of the guys who owned it and he pointed to the local shopkeeper, who had three children all under five. *Perfect.* My plan was hatched.

I sat down with him and said, "Let's make a kindergarten." He said it was a great idea, but where would it be. I said, "That building over there, directly opposite your shop. "How much will you give me for the lease?" he asked. I said, "I will make the building nice, I will pay for two teachers, I will hire two cooks to make the kids breakfast every day, and we will buy everything from your shop and not the other shop in the village. Once people know you have given this shop to me for one year, then everyone will come and buy their provisions at your shop, because you are such a kind man." You could see him, thinking and counting the Kwacha. He said, "Deal, when can we start?"

At this stage, I had no money. Well, I had some, but not enough to start this little venture. I decided to put the plan into action. I emailed two good friends back home in Scotland and told them the story, and asked if they would be willing to help. They suggested they would run the Glasgow half marathon and raise some funds." "Excellent," I said.

They raised $2000. I was ecstatic. I couldn't wait to tell the shopkeeper. I was telling everyone in the village and spreading the word about the kindergarten, we decided to hold a meeting and invite all the parents that had children, between 3-5 to join the Balagombe School, a new learning center for the kids. Nothing would prepare me for what was about to happen.

On the morning I wandered round towards the shopkeeper's house, I could see a huge crowd had gathered. As I approached I could see the shopkeeper, smiling away. It had already started, people spending their hard earned cash in his shop.

I promised every child a uniform and free schooling for one year. 84 kids signed up - it was amazing. I went to the albino seamstress and asked if he wanted some business. No one would give him any, as they thought he was freaky. He was delighted, I gave him a target of 30 uniforms a week and if he made all in two and half weeks, I would double his price. He reached his target, I don't care how he or what, but he made the target.

I also made uniforms for ten orphans from the senior school and paid for a year's uninterrupted education for them. I paid for five children from the private school, which had orphans also. I was like the pied piper. I will never forget the day I went to pick the money up from WU and Martin the country manager asked me what I was going to do with all of this money. I just replied, "Don't insult me by asking for any of it." I spent the remainder of the cash on some sports equipment for the school and bought a new football strip for the team.

What I got for this money is as follows;

Two teachers

Two cooks

84 children, with uniforms.

1 meal a day for each child, for a year.

Building painted and two black boards

Playground and fence

15 uniforms with school fees paid for one year

New football strip, with five training balls.

Various items of sports equipment for the schools.

I will always maintain if you go through the right channels, the aid will reach the needy and you will feel a lot better. I never donate money to NGO's, as only about 10% actually will go to a project. Why do you think these NGO get paid hardship allowances, drive big 4x4 vehicles, and live in beautiful colonial houses and have bodyguards? I never once felt threatened in Malawi.

Champions league Final 2005

If you witness a major sporting occasion, it stays in your mind for years to come and you can always remember where you were and what happened on that particular evening.

For the people who know me, I think they will all answer the same question if you were to ask them if I drink a lot. They will all answer, I can count on one hand the times I could say he was ever out of control with a drink.

This event is one I have always watched since I fell in love with the beautiful game. I only wish I could have seen Celtic lift their trophy in 1967. What a night that would have been. Everyone likes underdogs and that was certainly memorable. Liverpool v Ac Milan would certainly be a game that stuck in people's minds. Can you imagine, as a supporter, going through such emotions?

The stage was set. I decided to treat myself to a night in the big city. I booked into this hostel called the 'Korean Garden' and went to the expat sports bar and settled to watch the game. I saw these two Irish guys and asked if I could join their company. They obliged and we watched the game. As things were panning out and Liverpool was losing, 3-0 at half time, you can only imagine the manager's team talks, they would have been so contrasting.

I walked up to the bar to order my 3rd bottle of beer and was met at the bar by a very attractive Malawian lady. She spoke very good English. I asked her where she worked and she said she was visiting her cousins, who were also attractive. I suggested they joined us for the second half and they were quite happy to join our company. The Irish guys were beaming wanting to know why they would want to join us. I just said, "They want male company, doesn't mean anything will happen, does it?"

The game was an epic. I will always remember the game, but as what was happening the rest of the evening, I will put it down to instinct and experience.

I had six beers and that was about my limit, not that I was drunk, but I just knew when to stop. The two Irish guys said they had enough and were leaving to go back to the security and comfort of their colonial home. The well-spoken Malawian women asked if I would you like to go to Pirates (local night club). I said I would, but I had to go to the toilet first. She asked if I wanted a drink. I thought for a minute and said, "Vodka and coke." I was sipping the drink and the girls said, "Let's go." I knocked it back and quickly went to the toilet and as I came out, I felt a warm flush coming over me. I thought it was the alcohol kicking in. It was during our drive to the club, music blaring and the girls singing and screaming in the car, speaking in Malawian, that it started to hit home. I felt like I was slipping in and out of consciousness, the girl looked at me and kept asking if I was ok. I just about remember the neon lights of Pirates. They were becoming very blurry. I held on to the girl and we entered the club. I stood at the bar and my head was spinning, I said hold on one minute I needed to go to the toilet.

I bolted out of the fire exit, staggered to a taxi, and was slipping in and out of consciousness on the journey to my accommodation. It took me all of my time to stay awake for the five-minute journey, but I did. I went into the room, closed the door, and slumped on the bed. I woke up exactly 12 hours later. I have never experienced the effects of what I presume was a date rape drug and would never wish it on anyone. I am glad I had the sense to bolt for that fire exit or who knows what would have happened?

There was no point reporting this to the police, as I would have ended up paying more to file a complaint. That's how things work in third world countries.

Lake Malawi

If you ever get the chance to go there, then don't hesitate. It's a vast open lake where you cannot see the horizon. It's a tourist destination and the first stop for overland trucks that venture from Cairo to Cape Town, a popular venture for gap students. Every two weeks, a truck would venture there and it was a great place to spend the weekend, as many of these trips had lots of single girls, 70 % of these travelers were rich girls from all over the world getting off on an adventure across Africa. I couldn't understand it personally, you only ever spent two nights in one country and you were whisked off in the back of a truck, never having any time to witness the wonderful sites, which Africa had to offer you.

I was talking with the truck driver and he said it was the best job he has ever had and he wasn't particularly good looking. He said he was sleeping with nearly every girl as they would generally come into his tent, frightened because they thought they heard wild animals. I mean everything was surrounded by razor wire, how could this be possible?

There was a concert that particular weekend. It was the lake of stars concert and around 3000 people attended. One particular artist was brought to my attention, a musician called Wambali. He was like the James Brown of Africa. His band made this guy tick. I found out he was the only African at the time to be nominated for a coca cola award, a feat in itself.

A few days after the concert, I was down in Lilongwe. I went to the local bookstore, as I needed to look for another book to read, when I looked across the library, I saw this beautiful looking women staring at me. I caught her eye and she kind of shied away into the library and then went into the hairdressers. I never pursed it, I went out and crossed the street and went into the Internet café and was sending some emails. Around 10 minutes later, she walked in and sat next to me. She was browsing her mail also. I then made some small talk and asked the usual; name, occupation, where she lived, because her color wasn't the deep dark Malawian, it was a beautiful light brown color. I thought, *I hope this isn't another date rape*. I asked her if she would like to go for a coffee, but she had a prior engagement. We arranged to meet the following Saturday and I said, "The problem is, I have to go back to my village as we only have a few hours before darkness. I didn't want to be eaten by hyenas." She said it was ok, I could stay at hers.

As the Saturday approached, I decided to keep things quiet in the village. No point telling anyone your business. They just start to get even nosier. They already wondered why I was not married. I just said it's not that important where I come from.

On the day we met, it was just like any other day in the village, people sitting in the same places asking the same questions, like 'where are you going'. I just used to say somewhere over the rainbow. "Oh ok," they replied, "I know where that is!"

I set off walking into the bush, taking the usual route, walking by the usual houses, seeing the same people, wondering to myself, what a life they have. It must be like a time bomb, wondering if you were going to become infected with this terrible disease. I stood waiting on the roadside waiting for a pickup truck to take me partially into town. As the truck pulled up, I sat next to a well-dressed gentleman; with his shoes so shiny you could see your reflection in them. He asked me if I wanted to sit further forward, as I was moving forward and switching places. At the next stop we were greeted by a man taking his pig to the Saturday market, the pig was tied up at the back of the truck, right beside the guy's shiny shoes. 5 minutes into the journey the pig shit all over the guy's shoes. I thought he was going to kill the owner, it was so funny. We stopped at our mini bus lift, which was around 15 minutes from town, this was an area where there was so much wheeling and dealing going on, little bits of business here and there. The thing about Africa, nothing runs to plan, you would ask when does the bus leave, there was no answer, it could range from 10 minutes to 3 hours depending on whether the bus was full or not. The only time this did not happen was when you were leaving town. I guess it was their way of controlling the traffic in the city.

I went to the coffee shop where we had arranged to meet and there she was, on time and looking really lovely. We had a coffee and a chat and we went to see a nice suburb in Lilongwe. She had just bought another shop and was in the middle of renovating it. She was on the phone and was talking to this guy, she said he was her business partner and that she knew his wife really well as they went to her church. It was just small talk, so I never took much notice. After looking around, she asked me if I would like to go back to her house. Of course, I said. It was in the car when she said her daughter was on the way home and she had some friends with her. I went into the house and her young 16-year-old daughter came inside and said hello. She also was a very attractive and you could see she had her mother's good looks. We ate and we watched a movie and she snuggled up next to me on the sofa and said, "What time will you go back to the village tomorrow?" I said, "Possibly the morning." She asked me if I would like to go to church with her, she said it was a born again Christian church, blah blah blah. As I have no interest in religion, it didn't bother me in the slightest what it was. I leant over to kiss her and she turned away. I wondered why the rejection, but I always stuck to the same morals, if a girl rejected you on the first kiss, then don't force it, as she is certainly not ready for more than a kiss. My mother taught me this and I always stuck with it. She said sorry for not kissing you but I love someone else and when the time is right, I will love someone and kiss him, because my savoir understands. *What a load of bullshit*, I thought to myself. *Why can people think like this, it's not normal*!

I asked her who she was in love with. She said, "Jesus of course, who else?" She believed she gave her heart to him and when Mr. Right came along then Jesus would understand her beliefs.

I went to sleep on the sofa thinking, *what is it about people with imaginary friends*? I mean how could you believe in something that no one for sure saw or even existed?

I woke up with the usual cocks crowing. Even when you are in the city, people still seem to keep chickens, was it a sign of wealth. Definitely was a pain in the arse getting woke up at the crack of dawn every morning.

I heard this sweet voice coming through from the kitchen. She asked me what I wanted for breakfast. I replied some eggs and cereal, and then she hit me with this real clangor,

"Would you like to come to church with me?" I hesitated for a while and said, "Of course I would." I wanted to see what all the fuss was about and maybe try to work out what religion really meant to these people. As we approached the church, I saw many people dressed in their Sunday best and looking really like they were going to a wedding, again its all a show. I went in and there were so many happy people, whites, colored, black all mixing and glowing. I noticed a guy not too far from me, he seemed familiar, I was curious to know where I had seen him before, I asked where have I seen that guy before, she said, "That's Wambali." "Wow," I replied. I couldn't believe he was a member of this congregation. As the service started, the pastor said, "Are there any new people in the congregation today?" She looked round and said, "Put your hand up!" I asked what for and she said, so you can acknowledge you are new! I looked around and saw two others raise their hands, so what the hell, mine was up too. The pastor said, "Ok, I want you to go over and greet the new people to our congregation." I guess this was some way of bonding, but it was another way to piss me off, as I didn't really like that kind of influence. As the sermon went on, I was getting more and more bored, all the happy clapping wasn't my cup of tea, I just wanted this to be over. Then I was hit with another curve ball!

It was the last hymn and she turned round and said, "This is the chance for you to go and meet Jesus." I was confused. The hymn finished and the pastor, along with his other disciples lined up and he said, "Ok, who would like to come and discuss any problems they have had during the week and we will talk to god and he will give us the answers." What a load of bullshit. She asked me, "Would you like to go down and meet Jesus?" I hesitated, *should I go down*? Was this the chance to get my wicked way with her? No, I stuck to morals and said, "I am sorry, I can't see a man with a long white robe and a beard, so I don't want to talk to Jesus, today is not my day. I came here just to please you, not to worship the ground you walk on." If I had gone down, who knows what road I would have gone down and where it could have lead me? Maybe I wouldn't be sitting here writing this book, with a beautiful Indonesian wife and kid.

I think after this episode I thought to myself, the more I think about religion the more it annoys me and for people to lead their lives by it, I will never understand.

As I made my way back to the village, I was followed by a group of young kids. When I stopped, they would stop. It was like a cat and mouse game, I wondered what they were thinking and what they had in store in the way of life. How can a country so full of poverty develop, how can the people develop if NGO's were stealing all the money and putting very little back into the country?

Goodbye Malawi, hello Durban

The one good thing about leaving Malawi was the adventure ahead and travelling to meet other DI's, working our way down through Africa, and meeting many interesting people along the way. I was travelling with three Hungarian guys, they were all different characters. Character one was the joker of the pack and was the one I could relate to the most. He was sharp, funny, and always wanted to get up to mischief. Character two was quiet and reserved and extremely vociferous when he was drinking. Character three was funny in his own way and had a dry sense of humor, a pleasant guy, someone you could trust.

As we travelled down the east coast, our first port of call was Mozambique; a beautiful corner of Arica, colonized by the Portuguese and you certainly could see the influences. The building in Maputo, once would have stood tall and proud, but you could see the great divide in some areas of the city. We visited the Humana base there, the pretty Lebanese girl, whom I met at the college, was based there. We thought we would surprise her. When we arrived, we found the camp was under quarantine, an outbreak of typhoid, which was controllable if people washed their hands. I asked where she was; she had gone to town and was to be seen at her usual sandwich shop. I looked through the window and there she was smiling, but on the phone. I waited till she went off the phone, but that seemed to take forever, then she called me in. She was in deep conversation with her boyfriend, yes they had got back together and she didn't seem happy. She must have told him I was there. He got pissed off and she handed the phone to me, he hung up before I had a chance to say anything. I could see she was angry, perhaps not the time to be talking. I could tell she was premenstrual. What is it with women and their hormones? I can't believe women let themselves go under the control of mind, I guess something we men will never know. I asked her what she was doing that evening, she said going back to the accommodation. I waited for her to ask me if I would like to visit, I guess for old time sake! No response. I said my goodbye gave her a hug and met up with the lads, we stayed in a B&B and the next day we took a long bus ride to Swaziland.

Once you start to travel through SA, you begin to see the real vastness of the country; how it would take you days to travel through it and how much of an adventure it would actually become.

As we arrived, the first thing we did was look for a place to stay. We were on a budget, though my budget was a little more flexible than the other three. I always liked to keep some extra for such luxuries. I didn't mind helping the guys out, but I certainly wasn't going to pay for their accommodation.

The one thing that surprised me about Swaziland was it was pretty developed considering the country was ravished with AIDS. The place was awash with color. They do like colorful dresses and clothes, the houses were quite unique also, and staying in a country like this would certainly appeal to me. The people were very friendly.

The next destination was another bus ride to Durban, the eastern cape of SA and the first real modern city we had been in for six months. We were to write about our adventures and assist other development instructors in the school and back in the UK. We were supposed to stay there for at least three weeks, basically the longer you stayed there the less money the project spent on you. I said to the guys after the first week, let's work day and night and we can perhaps leave this school in 2 weeks, which gives us more time to continue our adventures. The tutors were saying, "No need to hurry your work, you have plenty of time." I worked it out. If they could keep us here an extra week, they, too, would be on a greater bonus. One day I had finished one of my projects and I asked one of the Hungarians, "Would you like to come into the city with me?" He said yes and went back to his room, and then he appeared with the other three and said, "Why don't we stay in town and we can come back on Sunday?"

After all, we had the weekend off. I was in an Internet café and saw that Celtic was playing Rangers that weekend. What were the chances of it been shown as I walked along the beachfront with the guys. I looked across and there was an advertisement for the game at a bar called Joe Cools. I was jumping up and down with excitement. I would get to see the game after all. As the sunset drew closer, the guys turned to me and said they were going back to the school. I couldn't believe it. I was stranded in a way; I had to find some accommodation, fast. The beach front in Durban is a very dangerous place and as the night drew ever closer, you could see the weirdo's coming out, waiting for vulnerable people like me. Of course, they wouldn't approach someone in a group, but on your own you are a sitting duck.

I saw a taxi and I asked the driver to take me to the nearest backpackers. As he sped out of town and drove further away from the city center, I could see the meter going up and up, I was so pissed. I asked him to turn back; I would pay him a lesson. I asked him to take me back to the original place where he picked me up. This time it was really dark. As I pulled up to the side of the pavement, I jumped from the car and ran as fast as I could, up this one-way street and out of sight. I walked into this bar called the London bar and asked the barman, can you tell me where the nearest backpackers were. He just looked at me and burst out laughing, as if to say you are crazy. There were another two people in the bar. I said f**k you and walked from the bar. I was walking down this street and saw this place in the distance. I walked through the door and I met this good-looking receptionist and she greeted me with a northeast of Scotland accent. I said, "Fit like," and she almost fell from her seat. She asked me how I got there and what was I doing on my own at this time, as it's very dangerous. She showed me a map of the areas not to go down of which I had went down all the bad routes. As she was about to give me the keys to my room, a Swiss couple walked into the hostel and said they had been robbed at knifepoint. The guy looked shell shocked. I said the best thing to do was cancel his credit cards and ask some friends back home to transfer cash through western union. The Scots girl was dealing with them and she felt really sorry for them. She asked them if they wanted to come out for a drink after her working hours. I asked, "Would it be possible for me to come also?" I have never been shy at moving forward. She replied, "Of course you can, let's all meet down here in two hours."

I checked into my room and was lying on the sofa. I hate lying around doing nothing. I always like to be up and about. I lay there tried to sleep for 20 minutes then I decided to get up and go and have something to eat. After eating, we all met in the lobby and the Scots girl ordered a taxi and off we went, the four of us. We arrived at this social club. It wasn't the greatest atmosphere, so I decided to say to the Swiss couple, imagine running away from your wife or girlfriend as you were getting mugged. They were getting more and more pissed off with my statements. You could see they didn't have time for my Scottish humor.

The next morning I went to watch the old firm game of which we lost. When I look back, I say to myself, what a waste of money that whole weekend was. I got very little out of it. You could see the Hungarian's mentality, save the cash for the rest of their travels. When I got back to the school, I found I was getting more and more agitated, wanting to leave, I spent most of the time planning the next leg of our journey. We had one more weekend to kill. I said why not visit another country; let's go to Lesotho, which was around five hours from Durban in the Drakensberg mountains.

As we were travelling there, we could see our time getting less and less. We arrived at the bottom of the Sunni pass and we still had a few hours of walking to do. I said, "Don't worry guys we will make it on time." The guys looked at me as if I was stupid and said, "How do you work that one out, Ron?" I said, "No matter where you go in the world someone will recognize this Celtic top am wearing." Ha ha, they replied. Sure as death is a hairy beast, this guy drove past in his pick-up truck and did a double take. He stopped and rolled his window down and in his broad Glaswegian accent said, "Where the hell do you think you are going?" I looked at the guys and said, I told you. They jumped in the back of the truck. I could see them in the mirror shaking their heads in disbelief. It turns out the guy was a Rangers fan. I am not sure if I were in his shoes I would have returned the favor. We spoke about football and what we were both doing in Africa for the whole journey. The guy, fair play, went out of his way to take us to a B&B.

The next day, as the dawn broke, we were having breakfast and I was looking through some tourist brochures. We were planning the next two days of the trip, golf, and visit the highest pub in Africa and visit a traditional Lesotho village. We decided to play golf first. Well, two of us did. If you ever get the chance to visit the Drakensburg Mountains and play a game of golf, then this is the spot, where you look into the distance and see almost flea-like vehicles making the journey up the Sunni pass.

It wasn't the greatest game of golf I'd ever played, but perhaps one of the most scenic, as we sat in the clubhouse drinking a coffee, the other two guys ventured into the café, we were leaving in an hour in a tourist bus to go up to the highest bar in Africa, as we were going up the winding road, I couldn't help but notice the steepness of the ravines. I bet many forms of transport have come a cropper down those hills. As we arrived in the bar, we were met with some other tourists. We looked over the edge and for a far as the eye could see there were rolling hills and beautiful countryside. This was certainly a place I could visit again. I sipped on my beer and thought, travelling and seeing the world is certainly a life for me. I was wondering what I should do when I arrived back in the UK, as much as I loved Scotland, I needed to get out. It wasn't so much the country; it was the town I was born, bred, and brought up in that was the issue. Of course, there are sometimes you miss it, but it's for about five minutes. The next port of call was the Lesotho village. I was confused why there were two houses, next to each other. The guide explained the women have the major role in the Lesothoian household. They have the large house and the husband has the small, if he wants to visit the house he has to knock on the door and ask the wife's permission, if she said no, then he has to sleep in his own house. A kind of weird culture certainly in Africa, but it seemed to work. It's amazing how cultures and religions rule people's lives, something I certainly wasn't brought up on.

We made our way down the mountain and we had one more night and we would be back in Durban, making ready for our next journey. I loved this part of Africa, slow and chilled, everyone just moving at their own pace, no pressure, but things managed to get done eventually. Slowly but surely.

Durban was around five hours away and on the way back one of the Hungarians suggested we take the blue train from Durban-Cape Town. This train would take almost two days and certainly would be an adventure, but what should we do for two days on a train?! I had a plan and I would run this past them when we decided.

I have never been a drinker, but one for celebration, yes. As we were entering the last two months of the program, why not celebrate? The journey as aforementioned was almost two days, so I suggested we buy a box of wine each and try to drink it before Cape Town. We all managed two thirds and that was mostly the first night, where we all got really drunk. One of the guys was becoming more and more aggressive with the alcohol, he was in the top bunk, and he rolled over and fell from the bunk smashing his head against the cabinet at two in the morning. I switched the light on, as I was on the bottom bunk. He woke up and said I had punched him; his friends said he was talking rubbish, which he was.

He then proceeded to spit in my face. I kept my cool and said to Norbi, the quiet one, I suggest you take him out before it gets ugly and we will all be thrown off the train. They weren't gone five minutes and Norbi came back and said this big black guy had Casaba by the throat, I had to go and diffuse the situation and Casaba was all apologetic and came to the carriage and fell fast asleep.

The next morning, another 12 hours from Cape Town, I was on my way to the buffet car for a coffee. When I stepped out of my carriage, there was an old colored guy coming out of his carriage at the same time and he saw me and quickly jumped back in. I waited as I knew he would pop his head out again, as he did I stepped in his carriage so the only way he go was out. I said, "Do you want to come for a coffee, my treat?" The guy was walking behind me and not ready for eye contact. As we spoke during the coffee he told me he was a pastor and that he was a political prisoner in Robbin Island, a prison were the great Nelson Mandela spent so many years incarcerated. What a waste of a great life. The guy told me I should visit, I told him I had been there almost three years ago and I already knew a little bit of the history.

When I began reciting some of the information, I could see the tears well up in the old man's eyes, he must have suffered so much mental trauma. He then asked where we were staying in Cape Town, I said beside the fort and he suggested the area was very dangerous and not good to travel around at night. He said he would show us an area upon our arrival and, true to his word, he did.

I wish I had more time speaking to the guy as am sure I could have had a few more inserts to this chapter, it was great how he held no grudges to the white man, especially the repression that was put upon him during his time on Robbin Island.

During our stay in Cape Town, we stayed in a Chinese bed and breakfast. The family wanted money every day, so staying there on a daily basis on a budget was not good. I wanted to pay it all up front, just so I wouldn't be hassled every day, but for some strange reason they wanted it paid daily.

Finally I had enough and I said I would move to another place, nearer to town just so I wouldn't be hassled. I met up with the guys on a few occasions, but decided to go to Robbin Island on my own. I could concentrate more and absorb more information. Although I had been there before, you always pick up information that you missed before. I really couldn't get my head around how people could hate so much, just because of the color of their skin.

South Africa is a beautifully dangerous country, with stunning scenery and a vast expanse of country. Travelling twenty-four hours on a bus from Cape Town to Windhoek, Namibia was an experience I chose to forget. Most of it was a night journey; the Hungarians were drinking vodka from a coke bottle and were almost left at a service station, as drinking on the bus was a big no no. Although we were in Windhoek only for twenty-four hours it was enough to see the European influence of the city. It was quite clean and modern. I did a few touristy things and was on the last leg of the journey. I was to spend a week in Zambia, working in a school for underprivileged children. It was far cry from the village of Balagombe in Malawi, the kids had a lot more to play with and structurally the set up was quite good.

We had a trip planned for whitewater rafting at the weekend with the ParQ trip. I was looking forward to this and I had the choice of a bungee jump off Victoria Falls or white water rafting. I had done bungee before, so I chose the latter. The trip started well, until we got to the climb down to the start of the Zambezi. I said to the guide, "This is quite dangerous." He replied many clients' trip's come to an end here, falling, breaking bones, and they are flown off in a helicopter. I tell you the descent was one of the most hair-raising experiences I ever did, but I survived the climb down and proceeded to the rafts. We were evenly spread throughout and given a good briefing, there were support canoes, which was reassuring. We set off on our 22 rapid adventure, the first 6 were reasonably tame, then the next 2 were fast flowing, as we approached rapid 8 we stopped and the women went in 1 raft and the men in the other, as we approached 9 the raft leader said the rapid was called the 'devil's toilet bowl' and the women ventured to the side and avoided the flush, I have never seen such a great expanse of water, flowing in directions that would make the Pentland firth look like a picnic, it spun us round and flipped us over. All I can remember was going underwater and coming out powerless 50 yards downstream. As I held on to one of the canoes, gasping for air and being ushered away from the raging torrent to calmer waters, I said to myself, "I am not getting in that raft again, I will walk the rest of the way."

The guide reassured me there would be only category 3's the rest of the way and there was no way we would flip again. If I chose to walk down, there would be a chance of me being taken by a croc, so I thought the better option would be the raft. It was defiantly an experience and I'm so glad I did it and received the t-shirt and survived the Zambezi and the crocs.

The next day, we went on the short 12-hour bus ride back to Lilongwe. We arrived back at 9pm. I jumped in a taxi and ventured to my 'Jesus loving friends house'. I planned to stay there for a week and, although it was free accommodation, she wanted more. I wasn't prepared to give her any more attention, as she was also a born again Christian and defiantly wanted me to be her new Jesus. This I wasn't prepared to do, I stayed there 1 more evening and wrote her a very nice note saying I wasn't the guy for her. She was very beautiful, but I'd had enough of Africa at this point and really wanted to get back to Scotland.

The next day we took a 6-hour bus ride to Blantyre and we met all the development instructors and had so many stories to tell of our adventure. We shared our experiences with the new teams and warned them of the perils of Africa, but to embrace the country with open arms. Malawi defiantly lives up to its name as the warm heart of AFRICA...

One day before we left, we went out for a meal and left the night watchman guarding our house. When we came back he was asleep and our baggage had been ransacked, I lost clothes and some personal things, but most importantly was my journal and diary which I had filled in every day, I felt sick from the heart as well as the stomach. I couldn't believe this was gone and all the memories were so hard to recall, I probably would have finished this book, before now, but I guess that's why it's taken me so long to write. As we travelled from Blantyre to Kenya, I left behind many footprints and still have the self-satisfaction of how it changed my life for the better.

I landed in Heathrow on the 23/ 12 / 04 and headed towards the National Express depot to catch a the bus to Leeds, where I would spend Xmas with my family .

I couldn't help take in the comments from kids 2 days from Christmas and overhear them saying, I want this that and the next thing, having lived within a poverished state for the last 9 months, It kind of sickened me of the cultural divide and the lifestyles and selfishness of the people of the UK.

I put my headphones on and listened to Wambali and dreamt of the warm heart of AFRICA and never took them off until I arrived in Leeds bus station, where my Mum and sister were waiting for me.

Back in the UK it was already too firkin cold, wet, and dreary, I really needed a new adventure and challenge....ASIA Beckons!

Pic 1: Orphans in the Garden after I bought some second hand toys, great to see happy smiling faces.

Pic 2: Everyday we had to walk a round-trip of 2k to collect water for our daily consumption.

Pic 3: My Pets Skippy and Larsson, I taught the children to respect the Dogs if they didn't they weren't allowed in the Garden.

Pic 4&5: Fundraised for the both of the schools I taught PE at, two friends raised money to give the children uninterrupted education for 1 Year. ($20 per child)

Glossary

After a few jars- a few pints of beer.

Afa hum oh piss- Smells of Urine

A fair drilling- Knocking really fast on the door

Azungu- white man

Bammfic- Banffer

Bams- Idiots or people who would do anything you ask them to

Bullies- People who terrorise others.

Backy- at the back of a main building

Banter- Having a laugh and a joke.

Blin him- Fight with someone and win the fight before it starts.

Bobbies- Police

Boobie traps- Where practical jokes would follow

Bottle of grouse- whisky

Breaker on the side- Someone interrupting a conversation and wanting to speak to who is ever on that wavelength.

Bread winner- Somebody who earns the families income

Booted him in the heed- Kicked him in the head.

Black Cat- When you try and out do each other, practical jokes

Barrie heat- Very Hot

Cloutie dumplings- Cakes

Chasies- kids running game.

Chippie- Fish and chip shop.

Chaser- shot of whisky.

Chored- Stole

CB- Citizen Band Radio or walkie talkie.

Chorrie- Steal something

Chumpa chump- Lollipop

Clanger- direct question

Choring- Stealing

Central Bar- formally known as Ma Black's.

Double whammy- Two way Prank

Drinking peeve-Having an Alcoholic beverage.

Deeking- Looking

Deek deek.- Have a look

Dyke- Wall or fence.

Ex SAS guy- A Man who only worked Saturdays and Sundays.

Egg him on- encourage him to do something.

Eating scran- Eating Food

Far you gan- Where are you going.

Fit do you care- Why should you care.

Fit like- How are you.

Fur rolled- Threw the guy over.

Garda- Irish Police

Gallowhill- A Street where most of the Characters and legends stayed.

Great rate of knots- going very fast.

Goalpoachers or Gloryhunters- Someone who would wait in the opponents half waiting for a goal scoring opportunity.

Giro Day- Social Security pay cheque

Homer- biased Ref

Half Decker- Half pint of beer.

Hipper- A pocket in the back of your trousers.

I ken- I know.

Kick a boot- Game of Football

Laddie- Young boy

Lassie- Young girl

Lino- Synthetic Vinal Carpet

Munter- Ugly person

Milkie- Milkman

Mannie- A Man.

Mercat Cross- Local monument.

Macewan's export- Local Beer

Nickets- Nothing

Nail Someone- Delibrately foul them.

Parkie- Field or small park area where you played team games on.

Rumble the Spoot- Stuff newspapers up drainpipes and set fire to them

Radar knob- A guy who looks for pussy anywhere and everywhere.

Ring- Ass

Reet teets- Practical Jokes or Pranks.

Reeking of strang- smelling of urine.

Rifled- Strike Something really hard.

Schoolboy error- silly mistake.

Shagged- had casual sex

Scalfed – lucky shot

Soccer- football, a game played prodomintely with your feet.

Squeeze box- Accordian musical instrument

Shag- Have Sex

Strang- Urine

Tosser- Not a nice person.

Tatties- Potatoes

Twickers- A sess pit of a Rugby Stadium.

Tournie in Bressie- A tournament in another Island.

Vanie- Vehicle that brought snacks to school.

Widies- A small forest at the top of our Town.

Wellies- Gum boots or Rubber Boots.

Woodbines- Cigerettes

Nisma- Maize Flour (porridge)

Acknowledgments: This book would not be what it is without the contributions of many people who each played an important role during the storyline @Stupatterson;@JohnLippe;@GeorgeLawerance;@JohnScott;RobScott@SpencerHenderson;@JohnMcHARDY@BillyPatterrson@RobbieConnell@BruceRennie;@GaryCox;@BarryWilson@JohnStewart;@GeorgeWebster(GeographyTeacher)@BanffRugbyClub;@BanffRovers;@RothieRovers;@WhitehillsFC;@AulFifefc;@DeveronvaleFC;@BanffSwimmingPool;@TurriffSportscenter;@TurriffSwiminingPool;

Special thanks to my mother Mary White who brought me up to give respect to people; Mandy White; Gillian White; Rosemary White; Kenneth White; James White and my extended Nieces, Nephews, Aunties and Uncles and anyone who knows me or knows of me.
Thank you the Pencil Princess (Fivver) who Proofread the book for me.
Big thanks to Antony Ritchie for designing his first e book cover.
Also, a big thank you to Local Photographer Francis Masson for the nice pictures from my hometown of Banff.
A special mention goes to a good friend of mine Gary Cox, who has endured a traumatic last few years since his beautiful daughter was diagnosed with Cancer, thankfully Abigail has this behind her and kicked the big C in the butt.
Finally I would like to mention my Beautiful Indonesian wife Ratna and our precious little daughter Kania.

46627508R00113

Made in the USA
Charleston, SC
21 September 2015